JN122853

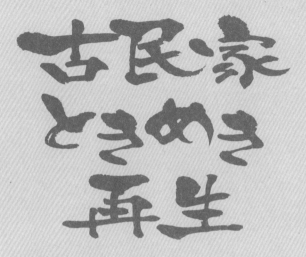

Wonder Renovation of
Traditional Japanese
Old Folk House

MIタウン企画部

片岡正治

MI Town Planning
KATAOKA MASAHARU

リーブル出版
LIVRE Publishing

天井を除き、天窓をもうける

物置を居室に変える

（上）２階建の土間物置を居室にし、一部吹き抜けにしました

まえがき

　現在、日本の景気は大きく低迷していますが、それは日本に限らず世界的な規模のようです。しかし一方で、日本は観光や伝統文化について世界的な注目を集め、高い評価を受けています。日本文化の深い精神性や細やかな細工や技術、日本古来の文化の素晴らしさは、国内よりも海外の人たちによって評価されはじめているのです。

　とりわけ注目が高まりつつあるのは、日本の在来木造住宅や伝統工法をふんだんに取り入れた「古民家」です。ごく最近まで、こうした建物は地震に弱くて危ないからといってほとんど解体され廃棄処分となっていたものでした。

　その流れは今も続いていますが、こうした歴史ある建物や古来からの伝統技術、日本人の英知などが消えていくかと思うと、何とももったいないと非常に残念に思っています。

　最近、古い民家の再生を相談に来られるお客さまが多くなってきました。

「100年以上の自宅を何とかしたい」

「田舎の民家を探してもらいたい」

「これくらいの予算で古民家を直したい」

「本当にこの値段で再生できるのですか？」

　みなさんがご夫婦で、それにおじいちゃんやおばあちゃんを伴って相談に来られます。そして、みなさんが古民家の話をすると目を輝かせて聞き入ってくださいます。

　古い物への愛着、ご自身や、自分の祖先の歴史が刻まれたお住

Preface

Japan's economy is currently experiencing a major downturn, but it seems to be also on a global scale, not just Japan. On the other hand, Japan is highly acclaimed for its international attention on tourism and traditional culture. The deep spirituality of Japanese culture, the delicate craft work and technique, and the splendor of old Japanese culture are beginning to be appreciated by people overseas as well as in Japan.

In particular, Japanese traditional wooden houses and "old folk houses", which have adopted many of Japan's traditional methods of construction, receive more attention. Until recently, most of these buildings were dismantled and disposed of because they were said to be vulnerable to earthquakes and dangerous.

The trend continues today, but I think it is very disappointing that such historical buildings, traditional techniques from the past, and Japanese wisdom will disappear.

Recently, more and more customers have come to consult me about the renovation of old folk houses.

"I would like to keep my house of more than 100 years old."

"I would like to ask you to find a folk house in the countryside."

"Can I really renovate it at this price?"

Many couples come to consult with me accompanied by their parents. They are listening to my story of old folk houses with their eyes shining.

When I feel my customers' excitement due to an attachment to old things, the joy of rejuvenating a residence with the histo-

まいが、蘇ることへの喜びでしょうか、私たちが内包する古来からの日本人の遺伝子が騒ぐのでしょうか。お客さまのそうした心のワクワク感が伝わってくると、私まで感動してしまうのです。

　美しく再生した古民家のある景色。日本の原風景への愛着、日本古来の文化や伝統を大切にする心の芽生えは、地域の魅力を一層輝かせていくことに繋がると私は考えています。

　だから工事を注文されるお客さまも、古民家を再生する私たちも、心をときめかせながら、再生工事を進めています。

　そこで私は、この再生事業の名称を『古民家ときめき再生』と名付けました。

　そして今回、今までのいくつもの感動のドラマをまとめて出版することにいたしました。

　この本を通して、読者の皆さまに少しでもその感動が伝わりますことを心から願っています。

2013 年 9 月

ry of ancestors, the ancient Japanese gene within us, I'm also thrilled.

I believe that landscape including a beautifully renovated old folk house, attachment to unspoilt landscape of Japan, a surge of empathy that values ancient culture and traditions of Japan, will lead to brighten local charm even more.

Therefore, we are working on the renovation of old folk houses together with customers who order construction with a shining heart and soul.

I named this renovation project "Wonder Renovation of Old Folk House".

And this time, I decided to publish a collection of the thrilling dramas I have had so far.

I sincerely hope that this book will transfer to the reader even just a little bit of the excitement that I have felt.

September 2013

目 次

Contents

語り尽くせぬ
古民家の魅力

The indescribable charm of
old folk houses

① 古民家との出合い

　私が古民家への情熱を持つに至った経緯をお話しするには、若かりし頃まで時間を遡らなければなりません。

　あれは、1982年（昭和57年）のことでした。

　当時の私は31歳でした。ギラギラとした青年建築士として、毎日必死で仕事をしていました。そして、暇な時間を見つけては、毎日のように、個人のお宅を借りては、仕事関係や地域の仲間たちと会議や集会を行っていました。

　つい話に熱が入って夜遅くなったり、休日の朝早くから集会を開いたりと、心苦しい思いで個人のお宅を使わせてもらっている状態でした。

　ある日のことです。仲間の一人から、

「自分たちで自由に使える会館がほしい」

という声があがったのです。

　そんな話を進めるうちに、解体する古い家の古材をもらってきて、それを自分たちで組み立て、自由に使える会館を建てようという話になりました。その後の管理や、建設に伴う資金のことなどは、全く頓着していませんでした。

　さて、若い高校生から、最高齢31歳の私までの、総勢15、6名の青少年が、日曜日にトラックを借りてきて、高知市内の古家を解体し、その廃材を瓦に至るまで、私の事務所の裏庭に運んできました。

　そんな話が周辺の方々に伝わり、

「私の鉄骨の家も壊すから、これも使ってください」

という温かい配慮もあって鉄骨の廃材も数多く集まりました。

　おかげで、私の事務所の裏は、会館を建てるための宝の素材ならぬ

① Encounter with an old folk house

I have to go back in time to my youth to share my experience of having a passion for old folk houses.

That was in the year of 1982.

I was 32 years old then. As a young aspiring architect, I was working desperately every day. And when I found time to spare, I borrowed an individual's house almost every day to hold meetings and conferences with my business associates and local colleagues.

I felt bad to borrow someone's house as we tended to carry on late into the night through passionate discussion, to be early in the morning and to hold meetings on holidays.

One day, one of my friends claimed, "I want a hall we can use freely".

As we discussed, we decided to build a hall we could use freely by ourselves collecting used materials from dismantled old houses. We didn't care about its management and fund-raising for the construction.

A total of 15 to 16 young people, from a high school student to myself, the oldest 31-year-old, rented a truck on Sunday, dismantled old houses in Kochi-city and brought the discarded materials, including roof tiles, to a backyard of my office.

The story was conveyed to the surrounding community. Due to warm consideration such as "Please use my materials also as I will dismantle my steel-framed house", we could collect a lot of steel frame waste.

Fortunately, the back of my office was filled with such waste materials: treasure materials for building the hall.

I was thinking that "As long as we collect waste materials, we

廃材でいっぱいになりました。

「廃材さえ集まれば、暇な時間を見つけて皆と一緒に組み立てていけば良いのではないか」

と何でも物事をストレートに考えてしまう性質の私は、そう思ったのです。

ところが、雨ざらしで木は腐り始めるし、周辺への話が広まり過ぎて、鉄骨などの廃棄資材を提供してくれる人たちが次第に多くなり、それに比例して、会館の完成を待ちわびる声が高くなっていきました。

「……これでは、何とか早く工事に取りかからねばならない……」

と、私はただ焦るばかりでした。

そのうちに資金も何とか工面がついて、やっと図面を書くことになりました。組み立てや建設に関しては同業者の方々にも協力していただき、ようやく会館の完成にこぎつけることができたのです。

この時に建てた会館は、今も若者たちに自由に使っていただいていますが、実はこの時に内装費用をできるだけ簡略化するために、カウンターや敷居鴨居など、あらゆるところに古民家の古い木材を使っていたのです。このとき私は、黒光りのする古い木材が醸し出す味わいに深い安らぎの波長を感じている自分を発見し、感動しました。

「この気持ちはいったい何なのだろう？　木材は古くなると人の心を安心させる深い味わいを持っているのではないだろうか……」

今にして思えば、この会館建設が私と古民家再生との運命の扉を開いてくれたのだと思えてなりません。

あれからもうかれこれ三十数年が経過しましたが、この何げない古木について味わった安らぎの気持ちが、これほどその後の私を古民家再生へと向かわせる熱情を生むとは夢にも思っていませんでした。

それなのに、いざ古民家再生を手がけ始めてみると、これほど奥深

would find some free time and assemble them together" due to my straightforward character.

However, wood started to rot in the rain and voices calling for the completion of the hall became higher as the number of people who provided waste materials such as steel frames gradually increased through word of mouth.

I was feeling uneasy all the time, "I have to start construction soon".

As we could raise funds, I finally got to make a drawing. With the support of people from our industry with regards to assembly and construction, we were finally able to complete the hall.

The hall built at this time was still freely used by young people. In fact, old wood from old folk houses were used everywhere such as counters and thresholds in order to streamline the interior cost. I finally found myself feeling deep relaxation in the texture of old shining black lumber.

"What is this feeling? Old wood may have a depth to reassure people's minds."

In retrospect, I can't help but think that the construction of this hall opened the door to my destiny and the renovation of old folk houses.

It's been more than thirty years since then, but I never dreamed that the peaceful feelings I had about this casual old tree, would create a passion for renovating old folk houses.

However, when I started working on an old folk house, I realized that there was no other job that had such a deep taste and so deepened my heart.

く味わいがあって、私の心を深めてくれる仕事はほかにないというこ
とに気がついたのです。

昭和 57 年栄光青年会館完成時の写真

Photo taken upon completion of the Eiko Youth Hall in 1982

② なぜ今、古民家が人気なのだろうか

古材で古民家の雰囲気を出した居酒屋

　大阪で大変人気があるという居酒屋に行ってみました。そのお店は
ごく普通のビルの地下にありましたが、ドアを開けてなるほど！と思
いました。「古民家風居酒屋」だったのです。満席でしたが、ちょう
ど入れ替わりで座ることができました。

　年期を経た黒い梁や柱、古ぼけたテーブルや椅子に触れていると、
何となく気持ちが癒やされ、温かさを感じます。おまけに、出てくる
料理やお酒が、なぜか美味しく感じるから不思議です。

　店内の状況はというと、相変わらず満席で、それでも次から次とお
客が来て入り口がいっぱいで、満席のためお断りをしている状態で
す。不況で客の入りが悪いと嘆いているお店が多い中では考えられな
い光景でした。狭いながらもこの古民家風の空間を求めて、人が続々
と集まってきているのだろうと強く感じました。

　このように最近、古民家の不思議なパワーは、いろいろな所に表れ

② Why old folk houses are so popular now

I went to a Japanese bar restaurant that was very popular in Osaka. The restaurant was in the basement of an ordinary building, but I was drawn in once I opened its door. It was an "old folk house style bar restaurant". The restaurant was occupied but I could eventually have a seat.

Somehow, I was healed and felt warmth as I saw aged black beams and columns, and touched the old-fashion table and chair. Moreover, The food and sake I was served tasted so delicious somehow.

The restaurant was still fully seated, yet the entrance was filled with guests arriving one after another. It was an incredible scene since many restaurants were lacking guests due to the recession.

I felt strongly that people were gathering to seek its old-folk-house style atmosphere, even though it was small.

In this way, the strange power of old folk houses has been demonstrated in various places. It creates unique charms to every living space such as housing, shops, offices, accommodation, hospitals and attracts people.

Depending on the various functions of old folk houses, it is possible to extract its forces through the way of using them. Especially, if you enter a real old folk house, such power is multiplied many-fold.

Recently, more and more people

てきています。

　住宅はもちろんのこと、店舗や事務所、宿泊所や病院など、あらゆる生活空間に独特な個性ある魅力を作りだし、その空間に出入りする人たちをとりこにしています。

　古民家は様々なニーズによって、活用の仕方ひとつでそれぞれの良さと持ち味を引き出していくことが可能です。特に本物の古民家に入ると、そうしたパワーが何倍にも膨らむのです。

　最近、古い持ち家を、再生工事をしたいという方が増えてきています。

　つい数日前もおじいちゃん夫婦と若夫婦が、お子さんを連れて再生中の古民家を見学に来てくださいました。その前日には、娘夫婦とおばあちゃんが3人で訪れ、工事契約をしていきました。

　古民家を再生しようというみなさんは、不思議なことに、ご家族そろって見に来たり、打ち合わせに来られたりします。これは一般的な新築工事では考えられない風情です。

　打ち合わせの内容も皆さんの希望も違います。そこでは持ち主さんが、古いお家を大事にしようという真剣さが痛いほど伝わってくるのです。

　古いものには、人をひきつける何かとてつもないパワーがあるように思います。そして、人を安心させるパワーも。

　当社を訪れたあるお客さまはこんなことをおっしゃっていました。

　「本当に気分が落ち着くし、この何ともいえない雰囲気は、味わったことがないのです。私は以前にハウスメーカーのお家を、言われるままに建てましたが、勉強不足だったので、その時は何でも新しいものが良いと思っていました。その後、家の事情でそれを手放し、今はアパート住まいですが、こんな良い古民家があるなら予算は少ないですが、ぜひ探してほしいです」と言われました。

want to renovate their old homes. A few days ago, an elderly couple and a young couple came to see their old folk house with their child. The day before, a grandmother and her daughter with her spouse visited us and signed a construction contract.

Those who want to renovate old folk houses come to see and consult with us together with their family. Such a gathering rarely happens in the case of general new construction works.

The agenda of each meeting and the expectation of customers are all different. But the seriousness of the owners who cherish old homes is conveyed strongly.

I think old things have enormous power to attract and soothe people.

A customer who visited my company told me, "I've never experienced such an atmosphere of relief. I used to build a major house builder's house. I thought anything new was good as I hadn't studied enough. I gave up the old house and lived in an apartment. Now, if there's a good old folk house, I would definitely like to ask you to find one although my budget is small."

The customer filled in the application form.

The other day, I made a contract with a customer who wants to renovate an old folk house of more than 100-year-old in Kahoku-town. The customer's house consists of 3 buildings, a one-story main building, warehouse, two-story earthen floor and second floor living room.

If you enter the gate of the house entrance, you will reach the front door. There was an outside veranda and a separate building with a series of small rooms to the east.

The house renovation will be done in three stages, including the gradual improvement of earthquake-proof reinforcement.

According to the customer's strong wish to renovate the ware-

そして、申込書に名前を記入していかれました。

また先日、香北町で100年以上の古い民家を改築再生したいというお客さまと契約をさせていただきました。お客さまの民家は、平屋建ての母屋と蔵と、2階建ての土間と2階部分居室の3棟からなっています。

屋敷の入口の門をくぐると、母家の正面玄関に行きあたります。濡れ縁があり、その東側の別棟には蔵に連続した小部屋がありました。

このようなお家は、段階的に耐震補強を合わせて改装工事を行っていくというように、3段階に分けて工事を行っていきます。今回は、蔵を改装して居室にしたいというお客さまの強い要望でしたので、蔵の利点を生かして、限られた予算の中でいかに古民家の良さを引き出すかというねらいで、工事を行うことになりました。

最近は若いカップルの方々で古民家を求めて訪ねてくださることが多くなってきています。

『すごくおしゃれで、心が癒やされる』『もう完全に新築よりも古民家です』という方が高知では着実に増えてきています。

こうした若い方の古民家志向は、今後全国に波及して次第に広まっていくことでしょう。

なぜ古民家が注目されるのか、その理由は数えきれないほどありますが、私は、古いものを大切にしてリフォームすることで、快適なゼロエネルギー空間が生まれるからではないかと思っています。

ゼロエネルギーとは、簡単に言えば、プラスとマイナスの力がちょうど押し合う部分に発生するバランスの良さと気持ちのよいエネルギーのことです。

古民家に居住する方にとって快適な空間になるのは、新しいものと古いものが生み出すハーモニー、つまり、年輪を経た樹木から発する明るく穏やかなエネルギーが、空間に満たされるための魅力によるの

house into a living room, we decided to carry out the work with the aim of taking its advantage and bringing out the goodness of the old folk house within the limited budget.

Recently, we have been receiving more young couples who are searching for old folk houses.

Those who mention, "So cool and soothing", "Old folk houses are completely better than newly built houses" are increasing constantly in Kochi Prefecture.

These young people's taste for old folk houses will surely spread gradually throughout the country.

再生後　香北町の蔵をリビングに活用　築後 100 年以上
Post-renovation Utilization of warehouse as a living room in Kahoku-town, more than 100- year-old.

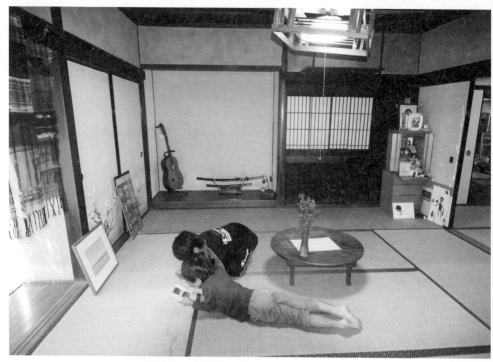

再生後の「淡路島の古民家」築後 100 年以上
100-year-old "old folk house in Awaji-island" post-renovation

かもしれません。

　木造建築は古ければ古いほど、素晴らしい再生古民家として蘇ります。それは今の新しい建築では表現できない歴史の味わい、奥深い落着きを持っているからです。そしてその古民家は、実際に見に来た方の心を魅了する不思議な力となっているのです。

　疲弊したストレス社会においては、明るくて美しい古民家の持つ力と癒やしの力は大きな魅力です。近年古民家ファンが増えている理由は、そこにあるのだろうと私は考えています。

　古民家の原点は日々の生活の喜びにあります。親子三世代が一緒に生活をする心強さと安心感、そして団欒の日々の楽しさ。そうした素晴らしさを再び呼び起こし家族の絆の大切さを教えてくれるのが古民家の力だと私は考えています。

There are countless reasons for old folk houses to attract attention. I believe that keeping and reforming old items will create a comfortable zero energy space.

In short, zero energy means a comfortable energy generating amid positive and negative power.

Old folk houses become comfortable spaces for those who are living in them since they are filled with harmony created by new and old things, namely, positive mild energy generated from aged lumber.

The older the wooden buildings, the better they will be revived as renovated old folk houses. Since they have a historical flavor which can't be expressed by current new architecture, such old folk house's magical power attracts the visitors' hearts.

In a stressful society, the strength and healing power of bright and beautiful old folk houses is a big attraction. I think that is the reason for the increasing fans of old folk houses recently.

The origin of old folk houses lies in the joy of everyday life. The reassurance and safety of living together and the joy of the three generations of a parent, a child and a grand child's daily lives. I think the power of old folk houses reminds us of such wonderful feelings and teaches us the importance of family bonds.

3 究極の住まいは木造建築

　古民家には新築住宅にはない風格と温もりがありますが、それはいったいなぜなのでしょうか。

　どうやらその秘密は木の存在そのものにあるようです。

　私が最も尊敬する住宅建築における師匠、「人間工学研究」の第一人者である小原二郎先生（千葉大学名誉教授、農学博士）が、こんな言葉を教えてくださいました。

　『木材は人間くさい材料である』

　これは古民家のすべてを表している名言といえるものです。

　少し長くなりますが先生の書かれた本の中からそれに当たる言葉を引用しましょう。

　『木は人間くさい材料です。今、1400年たった法隆寺の古い柱と、新しい桧の柱と、どちらが強いかと聞かれたら、『それは新しいほうさ』と答えるに違いありません。けれどもその答えは正しくありません。

　なぜなら木は切り倒されてから、200年から300年までの間は、強さや剛性がじわじわと増して2〜3割も上昇し、その時期を過ぎて後に緩やかに下降し始めますが、その下がりカーブのところに法隆寺材が位置していますから、新材よりもなお1割くらいも強いのです』

（『木の文化』小原二郎著　鹿島出版会より）

　小原二郎先生のおっしゃるように、古い家の木は弱くなったり、使

3 The ultimate residence is a wooden building

Old folk houses have a personality and warmth that new houses do not have, but why?

It seems that the secret lies in the existence of the tree itself.

Dr. Jiro Kohara (Professor Emeritus, Chiba University, Doctor of Agriculture), an authority of "Ergonomics Research", a master of housing construction I admire most, taught me the following words.

"Wood is a human-like material."

These words of wisdom represent everything about old folk houses. Let me quote such words from his book.

"Wood is a human-like material. If you are asked which is stronger, 1400-year-old columns of Horyu-ji (temple) or new cypress columns, you must answer "The new one". However, the answer is not correct.

Since the tree was cut off, strength and stiffness will increase by twenty to thirty percent 200 and 300 years later. After that period, it will begin to decrease gradually. Wood of Horyu-ji (temple) is located in the downward curve yet still about 10 percent stronger than the new material."

("Wood Culture" attributed to Jiro Kohara, Kashima publishing)

As Dr. Jiro Kohara mentions, old wooden houses are not getting weak nor useless but rather become harder and stronger after years and provide us "healing energy".

Photo by (c) Tomo.Yun http://www.yunphoto.net

えなくなっているのではなく、むしろ年月を経て硬く強くなり、また『癒やしのエネルギー』を私たちに与えてくれるのです。

　私は日本の住宅建築は木造建築だと考えています。日本は古来から木で家を建ててきましたから数十年前まではほとんどが木造住宅だったのです。それが日本人の心の温かさを育んできたと思っています。

　しかし戦後になって、多くの国民が自国の文化より欧米の方が優れていると考えたのでしょう。住宅建築の考え方が大きく変わりました。

　住宅は木造からレンガ造り、ブロック造り、鉄骨造り、鉄筋コンクリート造りへというように変化してきました。そういった歴史的な背景は、結果として家族制度の破壊につながり、社会に送り出される人間の基本となる家庭教育の破壊につながってきたのではないかと思います。

　現在の日本は核家族化し、一人ひとりが孤独になってストレス社会に埋もれ、不信と不安の中で暮らすようになっています。しかし、そんな時代だからこそ、これからの住まいづくりが非常に重要になるのです。人間は自然によって感化され、癒やされ、活力を充電できるのではないでしょうか。

　自然の中にいると、優しい心が蘇ってきます。木にはそうした自然の不思議なパワーが潜んでいるのです。

　近年になって自然との共生ということから、ようやく木造住宅の良さが見直されてきました。私にとってこれほどうれしいことはありません。

　これによってようやく人々が過剰なストレスから解放され、人を思いやる人間らしい住まいの空間で落ち着きを取り戻すことができるように変化していくことを信じています。

　日本の木造建築は世界で最高の素材を使い、そこに魂を込める深い精神性を生かす技術を持っています。それが世界に認識される日はもうそこまで来ていると私は考えています。

I consider the housing construction of Japan as wooden architecture. In Japan, houses were built with wood from ancient times so most of them were wooden architecture until decades ago. I think it nurtured the warmth of the heart of the Japanese people.

However, the view regarding housing construction changed significantly after the war as many people thought Western cultures were better than our own.

Housing has changed from wood to brick, to steel and reinforced concrete. I think such a historical evolution has led to the destruction of family systems, which in turn has led to the destruction of the family education, which is the basis of humans who are sent out into society.

Today, Japan has become nuclear families, where individuals have become lonely and buried in a stressful society, living in the midst of distrust and anxiety. Future housing construction becomes very important in such an era. I think human beings can be inspired, healed, and recharged through nature.

Being in nature brings back a gentle spirit. Trees have such a mysterious power of nature.

In recent years, the advantages of wooden architecture have finally been reevaluated in terms of coexistence with nature. Nothing could make me happier.

We believe that this will finally change the way people are able to free themselves from excessive stress and regain their serenity in a caring and humane living space.

Japanese wooden architecture uses the best materials in the world and has the skill to utilize a deep spirituality that puts the soul into it. I believe that the day when the world will recognize this is almost here.

④ 古民家をめぐる誤解

　高知を筆頭に、四国は古民家の宝庫です。しかし残念ながら、地元に暮らす方々にとっては、壊れかけた昔の古い家などは負の遺産にしか思えないというのも現状です。

　建築のプロの大工さんや設計士さん、工務店の方々に古民家の再生について尋ねてみると、大半の方々から次のような言葉が返ってきます。「こんな古い家を直すより、壊して建て直したほうがましですよ。これをリフォームしていたら、かえって高くつきます」

　こうした誤った考えが常識化しているのは、大変嘆かわしいことです。

　何より新築が良くて、リフォームや再生の工事は、新築以上にはなり得ないという価値観。それはちょっとおかしな考え方です。

　高知県香美市土佐山田町楠目の高台に位置した、築後 100 年以上はたっている物件がありました。

4 Misunderstandings about old folk houses

Kochi Prefecture is listed top among the Shikoku region rich in old folk houses. However, unfortunately, for the locals, half-broken old houses seem to be only a negative legacy.

If you ask professionals of architecture such as carpenters, architects and builder's office staff about renovation of old folk houses, most of them would get back to you with the following words.
"It's better to dismantle and rebuild a house than to renovate such an old house. It would cost more if you renovate it."

It is very sad that such wrong idea has become common sense.

There is a sense of value that new construction is good and renovation work can't be better than the alternative. I think it's strange.

There was a house more than a 100-years-old located on a hill in Kuzume, Tosa Yamada town, Kami city, in Kochi Prefecture.
At first, I gave up on the reconstruction because it was a terrible leaning house with one roof collapsing.

However, I couldn't help thinking about the remaining coal black round beams all the time.

I think the round beams might have been appealing to me to make use of them.

Before the renovation, the roof was falling off and the blue sky was visible as shown in the photo (1). The beams were corroded and dropped, the pillars had collapsed, the floors were falling out due to corrosion and termite's damage, which made it untouchable totally.

片方の屋根が崩れ、家は傾いているあまりにひどい家屋の状況だったので、当初は再生工事をあきらめていました。

　しかし、家に残っている漆黒の丸梁がなぜか心に焼きついて、工事をあきらめたというのに、私の頭の中には、ことあるごとにその梁が頭に浮かんで離れないのです。

　今考えると丸梁が、私に訴えかけていたのかもしれません。

　「私を生かしてほしい！　私の魅力を見てほしい！」と。

　再生前は、(1)の写真のように屋根は抜け落ち青空が見えているような状態です。当然、梁は腐食して落ち、柱は倒れ、床は腐食と犠害で抜け落ちていて、全く手をつけられない状態でした。

　(1)の写真は崩れた部分を取り除き、一部束補強を行った状態です。屋根がないので、床も抜け落ちていました。その部分は取り除きました。床も壁も屋根もない状態ですから、残った棟半分の部分の家は南側に大きく傾いていました。

　自問自答の末、匠の技を持つ何人もの大工とも、何度か協議を重ねてみました。答えは皆さんが「これはちょっと無理ではないだろうか。わしにはできそうもない」「この家はちょっと無理だろう。解体しかない」という、答えはそればかりでした。

　「再生可能な建物の限界はどこにあるのか？」という自問自答を繰り返していました。この答えを出す絶好のチャンスではないのかと思い、何とかできないかと具体的な課題や建築家としてのアイデアを示して再度話し合うと、「うん……それなら傾きは直る。梁も継ぎ合わせることはできるだろう」とやっと心強い返事が返ってきました。

　(2)の写真は、前述した崩れた部分をつなぎ合わせ傾きを直した写真です。こうして、古い部分と新しい部分とを組み合わせて、以前

(1)

The photo (1) shows the situation after removing the collapsed parts and fortifying some floor posts. Half of the house's floors were missing since there was no roof. I removed them. The remaining half of the house was tilted to the south.

After questioning myself, I had several discussions with many carpenters with craftsmanship.

Most of their answers were negative such as "This may be impossible. I don't think I can do it." "This house is impossible. There is no choice but to dismantle."

I asked myself repeatedly, "Where are the limits of renewable buildings?"

I considered this as the best opportunity to answer my own question and discussed again by pointing out concrete challenges and proposing their counter proposals as an architect.

I finally got a reassuring response, "Well... in such case, the tilt

とは違った新たな建物が出来上がりました。

　この物件は、工事途中から多くの方に注目されていました。工事の段階から、再生古民家の出来上がりを心待ちにしている方が数多くいらっしゃったのです。そして結局、なんと工事途中で購入者が決まったのです。

　古民家は一つとして同じ顔をしたものはありません。

　楠目の古民家は、古民家が独特な魅力と個性を持っていて、それが出来上がったときに周囲の自然環境と一体となって大きな風格を醸し出すことを教えてくれた貴重な物件でした。

　このような古民家は田舎のあちこちに数多くありますが、皆さんは再生を諦めて、解体したり、崩壊するまま放置しています。本当にもったいないことです。

　やがて朽ち果て、解体を余儀なくされる古民家。素晴らしい各地域の宝物が、簡単に消し去られていく。これは悲しい現実です。

　新しいものと古いもの。古民家はそれを改造すれば一層輝きが増すものだということを、もっと知ってもらいたいと強く思うばかりです。

　古民家の素晴らしさを一刻も早くわかっていただいて、大切に次世代に引き継いでほしいのです。そういう意味からも、古民家再生の見学会は、大きな役割を持っていると思っています。こうした機会の提供なしには、古民家の素晴らしさはなかなか理解できないのです。

　埃まみれでくすぶっていた古い梁も、心を込めて創り上げていくと、驚くほどおしゃれな雰囲気を醸し出してくれます。住まう人の感性と共鳴する個性溢れる美しい空間。そんな日本の宝物が、少しでも多く残り、それを地域の方々に知ってもらうためにも、古民家ときめき再生事業が地域の活性化にお役に立つことを願うばかりです。

too good to waste.

It is a sad reality that each region's wonderful treasures, old folk houses soon to be decayed, are forced to be dismantled and are easily removed.

I just want more people to know that old folk houses' remodeling of new/old will make them brighter.

I want you to understand the beauty of old folk houses as soon as possible and carefully pass them on to the next generation. In that sense, I think that a tour of old folk houses has a big role to play. Without providing such an opportunity, it would be hard to understand the splendor of old folk houses.

Old beams that were dusty and smoldering can form a surprisingly stylish atmosphere if created wholeheartedly. A beautiful space full of character that resonates with the sensibilities of the inhabitants. I just hope that our "old folk houses wonder renovation project" will help revitalize the region so that as many such Japanese treasures as possible will remain and appreciated by the local population.

⑤ 古民家再生の工夫と注意点

　古民家再生というと、よく「昔の家そのままの復元」と勘違いされてしまいますが、私たちが行っている再生工事は、そのような古民家ではありません。「古民家ときめき再生」というのは、「古いものと新しい技術と新しい素材の組み合わせで出来上がる」全く新しい古民家の意味だと思っていただきたいのです。

　私たちの再生工事では、古い家ほど快適で美しい味わいのあるお家に生まれ変わります。

　例えば、お風呂はユニットバスなど水仕舞の良い新設機器を使い、木が腐ったりシロアリの巣になったりするのを徹底的に防ぐ手立てをします。住宅環境は生きた木材の特質と自然のエネルギーや通風を取り入れ、生かすことによって、冬暖かく、夏は最高に涼しくなります。

　「古民家のときめき再生」は、日本の古き良き英知を生かし、現代建築の新しい技術と、人体にやさしい自然材料を駆使した、新しい住環境を生みだしていく工事なのです。

　例えば、再生しようとしている古民家の煤けた古材の梁。その梁だけを見ても、私にはそれが凄い価値を持つものだとわかります。

　古民家の素晴らしさや、木造住宅の良さは近年急速に見直され、多くの建築家の先生方も今では木造住宅の加工技術は最高レベルの域まで達しようとしていると評価されています。まして1400年たった法隆寺のヒノキの木が、新しい今のヒノキの木よりもさらに1割も強度が増しているという学会の発表は、まさに衝撃的で、木材がいかに強い材料であるかの証明になりました。

　今私が見ているこの梁も、100年という長い年月を、煙でいぶしていかないと、このような古材の梁にはなりません。この梁は強度も強

5 Ingenuity and precautions for renovation of old folk houses

When it comes to the renovation of old folk houses, it is often mistaken as "the restoration of the old houses as they used to be". However, what we are doing as restoration work is not such old folk houses. "Old folk houses wonder renovation" actually means totally new old folk houses "created in combination with old items and new technology and materials".

Our restoration work will transform the old houses into more comfortable, beautiful and tasteful houses.

For example, for baths, we use new equipment such as unit baths that are well-drained to prevent trees from becoming rotten with white ant nests. Housing environment will become warm in winter and super cool in summer by adopting and utilizing living wood features and natural energy and ventilation.

"Old Folk Houses Wonder Renovation" is a work of creating a new living environment by utilizing the good old wisdom of Japan, new techniques for modern architecture and human-friendly natural materials.

For example, if I look at sooty old beams from an old folk house we're trying to renovate, I can appreciate their great value.

The splendor of old folk houses and the goodness of wooden houses have been rapidly appreciating in recent years, and evaluated by many architects and experts so that the processing technology for wooden architecture is reaching its highest level. The stunning presentation by the academics showing that 1400-year-old Japanese cypress of Horyu-ji (the oldest wooden building in the world) is 10% even more tenacious than the new cypress, has proven how strong wood building materials are.

くなっていて、現在も強度が増し続けているのですから、まさに底知れぬ木のパワーを感じさせられます。

古民家は住まう人の個性によって、その表情もさまざまに変化してきます。

住みやすく、そして美しく見せるために、外部のブロック塀を少し低くして補強をし、棟瓦のがんぶりをつけて、土佐漆喰を塗る。こうするだけでも外見の表情は、ガラッと変わるのです。後は住まう方の感性次第で、空間や家の表情がさまざまな変化を見せ、他に同じもののない個性的な住宅になるのです。

古道具も古民家に置くと立派な生活のアクセントに変わります。

玄関に石うすを据えて、その中に水と水草を入れ、金魚やメダカを泳がせるのもいいでしょう。そこに竹や木でできた蓋をつけるとまた雰囲気が変わります。

このように、ちょっとしたことで趣のある涼しさや温かさを醸し出すことができるのです。古民家の空間には、日本の奥ゆかしい文化表現を楽しむ「粋な空間」がよく似合うのです。

何よりも古民家には、そのような創意工夫がよく似合います。

土間に古い軒瓦を埋め込んだり、壁天井を土佐和紙で仕立てたり、野の花を飾ったり。何げない心の表現が大きなおもてなしを生み出して、わくわくする瞬間です。古民家には、住む人のクリエイティブな気持ちを刺激する力が少なからずあるのです。

そういえば、どういうわけか古民家を求める方は、ほとんど前向きな人が多いのです。「木は、気を集める」と高知大学の田村教授から以前に教えていただきましたが、古い古民家などに包まれていると自分自身の未知の可能性を引き出してくれるのかもしれません。

さて、そんな素晴らしい宝物の古民家ですが、実は一つだけ大きな欠点があります。それは、再生前の古民家は、長い年月の間に家主の

This beam I'm now looking at wouldn't have become such an old wood beam if it had not been smoked for 100 years. The strength of this beam has been increasing even now. It makes me feel the profound power of wood.

The character of old folk houses changes in various ways depending on the individuality of its residents.

By slightly lowering the exterior block for reinforcement, attaching round semi-circular ridge-roof tiles and applying Tosa plaster, the appearance changes drastically.

The old tools also turn into a fine accent for living when placed in old folk houses.

Why don't you place a stone mill at the entrance, fill it with water and water plants, and let goldfish and killifish swim. Placing a lid made from bamboo/wood will change the air.

In this way, even a minor change can create an elegant cool/warm atmosphere. The space in old folk houses is well suited to becoming a "stylish space" where you can enjoy the refined cultural expression of Japan.

Above all, such ingenuity suits old folk houses very well.

This is a moment of excitement, with expression of the heart creating great hospitality, such as embedding old building tiles to an earthen floor, finishing walls and ceilings with Tosa Japanese paper, and decorating wildflowers. Old folk houses have the power to stimulate the creativity of its residents.

By the way, those who seek old folk houses are mostly positive people somehow. I was taught by Prof. Tamura from Kochi University that "Wood will soothe your mind". When you are surrounded by old folk houses, you may be able to unleash your unknown potential.

In fact, there is only one major disadvantage of such wonderful

再生後の「夜須川の古民家」縁側部分 築後100年以上
Veranda of a renovated "old folk house in Yasugawa"
over 100-years-old

管理が行き届かず、家を作っている木材が腐食や蟻害で初期の強度を持っていないことです。

これをそのまま放置しておくと、少しの衝撃で倒壊の危険があります。住まいの最大の役割は、住まう方の命や財産を守ることにあります。

そのためには、まず構造材を専門家に診断してもらって、劣化の度合いを調べて、まず補強工事を行うことが絶対に必要です。県や市町村からの補助金も出ていますので、その手立てを相談されるのが必要です。

耐震診断費用は本人負担3000円・耐震補強費用補助金設計費200,000円、補強工事費900,000円が受けられます。（高知県の場合・2013年8月現在）古いお家を新しい古民家に再生するために、命を守る手立ては万全にしておかねばなりません。まずはそのことを近くの設計事務所や工務店の専門家に相談することから始めなければなりません。

treasures old folk houses. Before renovation, old folk houses' wood materials have lost their initial strength due to corrosion and termite damage caused by the lack of landlords' house management over the years.

If this is left as it is, there is a risk of collapse. The greatest role of a house is to protect the lives and property of its residents.

For that purpose, it is absolutely necessary to have a specialist diagnose the structural material, check the degree of deterioration, and then perform reinforcement work first. There are also subsidies from prefectures and municipalities, so it is necessary to consult with them regarding these measures.

Seismic diagnosis costs are 3,000 yen while subsidies for seismic reinforcement costs and design costs are 200,000 yen, and the subsidy for reinforcement construction costs are 900,000 yen. (In the case of Kochi-prefecture, as of August 2013). In order to renovate an old house into a new old folk house, you must make every effort to protect your lives. You must start by consulting with local experts from design offices and builder's offices.

Although old folk houses have good old wisdom and atmosphere, there seems to be some limitation in terms of comfort, convenience, insulation and lighting for modern people due to differences in lifestyle.

Recently, a growing number of young people are requesting renovation of old folk houses as an optimal place for their grandpas and grandmas to protect their lives and nurture health and well-being. In such cases, "insulation" plays a very important role in the renovation.

The insulation is the most important thing in ceiling construction. Health, comfort, energy savings and safety of the residents are determined by the selection of materials.

昔の古民家は、古き良き英知や雰囲気は持っているものの、生活ス
タイルの違いもあって、現代人の快適性、利便性、断熱性や採光の点
では無理があるようです。

　若い方々から、おじいちゃんおばあちゃんが生命を守り、英気と健
康を養う格好の居場所として、最近では古民家再生工事を希望される
方も増えてきています。そのための大きなポイントは古民家の改修に
おいて「断熱材」がとても大切な役割を果たします。

　天井の工事で一番大切なのはこの断熱です。その素材を何にするか
で、住む人の健康、快適性、省エネ、安全性が決まってきます。

　こうした断熱材に、私たち建築家は、もっとこだわる必要がありま
す。高度な断熱処理は、快適性を左右する大切な部分なのです。

　特に屋根部分の遮熱断熱処理を誤ると、夏は暑いうえに冬は底冷え
がする。冷暖房が効きにくいので光熱費がかさみ、腐食と白蟻の温床
となってしまう住まいになるために注意が必要です。

　遮熱断熱材の役割はエネルギー消費をできるだけ少なくして光熱費
を抑え、なおかつ、室内と外部空間を融合すること、つまり外部空間
の室内への取り込みをして、家の立地環境を十二分に生かすことです。

　これらのことも含めて、深い経験を持つ古来からの『匠の技』の英
知は、古民家再生の重要なカギといえるでしょう。古民家再生には匠
の技が絶対に必要です。もちろん新築物件でも匠の技が大切なことは
言うまでもありませんが、古民家再生ではそれがより強く求められる
のです。

　この匠の技の腕次第で、再生古民家の姿は大きく左右されます。古
民家再生は、創り手の感性と匠の技、そして住まう側の要求と住まい
方で作り上げられていくのです。ここが新築物件と大きく違う所です。

We architects must be more particular about these insulating materials. Advanced insulation is an important part of people's comfort.

In particular, making a mistake in the thermal insulation treatment of the roof area will end up with heat in summer and very cold in winter. You must be careful because poor air conditioning results in high utilities cost and a source of corrosion and white ants.

The role of thermal insulation material is to minimize energy consumption and reduce energy costs, while also combining the interior and the external space, which means to integrate the external space into the room, thereby making full use of the home's location environment.

Moreover, the old wisdom of craftsmen with a deep experience is an important key to the renovation of old folk houses. The artistry of craftsmen is absolutely necessary for the renovation. Of course, it goes without saying that craftsmanship is important even for newly built properties, but it is even more strongly required for the renovation of old folk houses.

The skill of the masters will greatly affect the outcome of renovated old folk houses, which combines the sensibility and technique of the craftsmen, the demands of the residents and their way of living. This is a big distinction with newly built properties.

❻ 古民家のよろこび

　私は古民家の中でも特に、梁と古材の持つパワーに魅了されています。

　天井裏に隠れていた、ススで真っ黒になってすごい存在感を出している梁や柱です。

　洋室であれ、和室であれ、それぞれの良さを引き出しながら、自らの個性を存分に出している古い梁です。何度見ても、決して見飽きることはありません。

　そうした古木の梁や柱に並々ならぬ関心を持っています。それは、自身の建築哲学の一つに、

　『再生しようとする物件に対して一番にやることは、まず屋根裏を見る』

　という信念に基づいて行動した結果、一番先に自分の目に飛び込んでくる物が、この梁だったからでしょうか。屋根裏の梁を見た瞬間に、その家の新たな姿を予兆するかのように、私の頭の中にささやきかけてくるのです。

　屋根裏の梁はどれ一つ同じものはありません。10軒が10軒、20軒が20軒。まさに十人十色です。どれ一つとして同じ物がなく、匠の技の競いどころです。それぞれの家に個性があり、そこには独特の魅力があります。梁は古民家において魅力のかなめなのです。

　古民家に使われている古材たち。時の刻みを忘れさせてくれて飽きることがありません。それどころか、見れば見るほど、心の中に限りないエールを送り続けてくれ、力がふつふつと湧いてきて、心のエネルギーを充電してもらっているような気がします。

6 The pleasure of old folk houses

I am particularly fascinated by the power of beams and old materials of old folk houses.

The beams and columns hidden behind the ceiling are sooty black and have a great presence.

Even if it is a Western-style room, it is an old beam that brings out the excellence and fully expresses its own individuality.

No matter how many times you look at it, you will never get tired of it.

I'm deeply interested in such old wooden beams and columns. Since I've been taking action according to one of my mottos of architecture philosophy: "The first thing to do with a property you're trying to renovate is to look at the attic", such beams came into my eyesight first of all and whisper into my mind as if they were projecting their new appearance.

None of the beams in the attic are the same. Every beam is different. The technique of the craftsmen make a difference. Every house has its own character and unique charm. Beams are key to the charm of old folk houses.

Old materials used for old folk houses never make me bored and let me forget the passage of time. The more I see them, the more they keep sending endless cheers to my heart and recharge my heart's energy.

When investigating old folk houses, sometimes you can find such wonderful items. This is a plate discovered under a hole in a hill behind a thatched house in Motoyama-town called "Kitayama lodge, yuzu (citron) house" where residents disposed of broken bowls and plates etc. Believe it or not, 12 plates were discovered

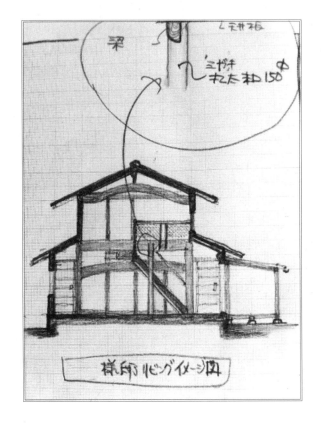

古民家再生の調査をしていると、時としてこんな素晴らしいものに出合えることもあります。本山町(もとやまちょう)の茅葺(かやぶき)の家『北山山荘・ゆずハウス』の裏山の大きな岩の下に穴を掘って割れたお椀(わん)やお皿等を捨てていた穴底(あなぞこ)の下から出てきたのが、このお皿です。無傷(むきず)で何と12枚が埋められていたのです。

古伊万里のさらに前の初期伊万里の皿です。土の中から出てきた時にはお皿の色もくすんでいましたが、時間がたつにつれ、つややかな光沢が現れはじめました。本当に素晴らしいお皿です。

花に戯(たわむ)れる蝶々(ちょうちょ)と、雪の結晶(けっしょう)を見事にアレンジして描(えが)かれています。デザインを技としている私たちも学ぶべき点が多々あります。そして、この模様。蝶の文様(もんよう)に、雪の結晶が描かれています。顕微鏡(けんびきょう)もない時代によくぞここまで書けたものだと感心します。お皿の裏面には高台があって縁取(ふちど)りの円、この寸法(すんぽう)の一つ一つも考えられての間隔(かんかく)でしょう。

お皿の中央にあるのが、銘(めい)ですが、渦(うず)の文様(もんよう)、周囲には唐草文様(からくさもんよう)と

intact. They are early Imali plates dating back even before the mid-Edo period of Imari-ware. When discovered in the soil, the color of the plates was dull. However, a shiny glaze began to appear over time. They're truly wonderful plates.

Butterflies playing with flowers, and snow crystals are beautifully arranged and drawn. There are a lot of things to learn also for us using design techniques. I am impressed by the design of butterflies and snow crystals from the period, without the use of microscopes. There is a base in the back with a border circle of examined size and distance.

There is a name in the center of the plate, a spiral pattern surrounded by arabesque patterns like a winding design in perfect balance. The spiral in the center is called a "spiral luck" written by abbreviating the character "luck".

From the feng-shui point of view, a spiral is a source of power also used at the Beijing Olympics. The winding design of arabesque pattens is said to symbolize the power of the dragon. Feng-shui is adopted in various ways by such old items. I feel healed and rejuvenated when I look at the item filled with stories of its creator. It really amazes me.

When I'm looking at a black sooty large wood beam from a hundreds of years old folk house, I realize its great existence that has been protecting residents' lives silently.

I feel like I'm encouraged by the beam "You'd better be proud of your work protecting a lot of people in contemporary life and doing your best simply with gratitude no matter what you are told or whatever happens."

There are many natural and unpretentious splendors in old folk houses. We also would like to live in such a way.

I often give my greatest gratitude to these old folk houses, who

でもいうのでしょうか、くねくねとした文様が、見事なバランスで描かれています。この中央の渦は、『福』という文字を略して書いた通称『渦福』と呼ばれています。

風水学的には、渦はパワーの源で、北京オリンピックでも使われていました。そして、唐草文様のくねくねした模様は、龍のパワーを象徴するものだそうです。こうした古いものには、いろんな形でこの風水学が取り入れられているのです。そうした作者の強い想いがこめられているのか、眺めていると癒やされ元気が出てきます。本当に不思議なものです。

数百年を経た、古民家の巨木の真っ黒にすすけた梁を見つめていると、ただ黙々と何も言わずに住まう人間の命と生活を守ってきた古民家の偉大な存在に気がつきます。

『現代の生活において、多くの方々を守る仕事に誇りを持ち、何を言われようと、何があろうと、あるがままに感謝しながら愚直に頑張っていくことだよ』と、梁に励まされている気になるのです。

自然の素晴らしさや、自然体の気取らない素晴らしさが、古民家には数多くあります。人の生き方もかくありたいものです。

私はよく、分け隔てなく、多くの方に幸せを与え続けているこれらの古民家に、最大の感謝をささげています。

感謝の思いとは不思議なものです。あらゆる所作や、物の配置にそれが表れるのです。古民家はそうした精神面の希望や勇気や、優しさを、光と影や色彩や古道具とあいまって的確に表現し伝えてくれるのです。

解体寸前のこうした古い民家でも、詳しく調査をしていくと、意外な宝物がここには詰まっているのです。隠された部分に心の目を開いていけば、その本質である素晴らしい形が見えてきます。

continue to give happiness to many people indiscriminately.

The feeling of gratitude is represented in every movement and arrangement of things. Old folk houses properly express such spiritual courage and tenderness through lighting, shadow, color and old tools.

Even in these old houses, which are about to be demolished, unexpected treasures are packed as we go through the detailed research. If you open your mind's eye to the hidden part, you will see its essence and wonderful form.

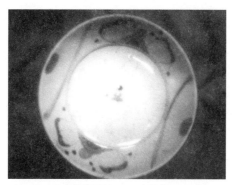

初期伊万里の皿　表部分
Early Imari plate, front side

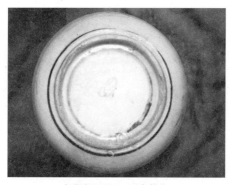

初期伊万里の皿　裏部分
Early Imari plate, back side

よみがえった古民家

Revived old folk houses

事例 1　天空の古民家

（2011年度ＴＨ大賞　リフォーム部門審査員奨励賞^{しょうれいしょう}）

　古民家の風格^{ふうかく}と温もり。その味わいのある空間はなぜできるので
しょう。その秘密は実は木の存在そのものにあるのです。ここでは実
際にわが社が手がけた古民家をご紹介します。

　TH大賞リフォーム部門審査員奨励賞をいただいた建物。これは、
私が『天空の古民家』と呼んでいる古民家です。
　場所は高知県いの町吾北村^{ごほくむら}の山頂^{さんちょう}近く、築120年以上はたってい
る古民家でした。この古民家は、空気の澄^すみきった美しい空の下、鳥
たちの鳴き声に包まれていました。日常生活の疲れをすべて吸収して
くれるような、神聖^{しんせい}な環境の中に立っていたのです。
　この「天空の古民家」は2010年に完成したのですが、その翌年
の2011年に、TH大賞リフォーム部門審査員奨励賞を建築家の清水
文夫^{ふみお}先生のご推挙^{すいきょ}で受賞することになったのでした。

　私はこの「天空の古民家」に立った時、いろんなことを考えさせら
れました。
「騒々^{そうぞう}しい社会に埋没^{まいぼつ}することなく、たまには自身の人生を高い位置
から見下ろしてみてみることも必要ではないのか？」

Case 1 Old folk house in the sky

How can you create a space with the flavor of dignity and warmth of the old folk houses? In fact, the secret lies in the existence of the tree itself. Here, I would like to introduce some old folk houses which our company actually worked on.

The building was awarded the TH Grand Prize, Reform Division, Judge's Encouragement Prize. This is an old folk house which I called "Old folk house in the sky".

It was a more than 120-years-old folk house located nearby a summit of Gohoku-village, Ino-town, in Kochi Prefecture. It was

そうした心境にさせられました。

ここにいると、ふと何かを悟ったような気にさせられるのです。

そんな古民家の再生で、審査員奨励賞をいただいたのですから、なおさら深い喜びを味わったのは言うまでもありません。

右頁は、『天空の古民家』の再生前後の外観です。

再生前には木材は腐食し、シロアリの被害に遭っていました。ほとんどの方はその状態を見て、この建物は解体以外に方法はないと考えるに違いありません。しかし私の仕事は、それを再生させようと考えるところから始まります。

この状態をどう再生すれば、古民家の木々たちがささやきあい、喜びの声を掛け合い、輝きはじめるか。住まう人の心を癒やし、感動を与えることができるのか。それを徹底して考えながら模索し始めるのです。

その結果、再生後は、あのみすぼらしい古民家が、このように立派に変身してしまいました。

まさに古民家の木々たちの喜ぶ声が、聞こえはじめた瞬間です。

この重厚な梁を見てください。数十年前の梁が蘇ったのです。人が住み、木も輝きを放っています。これらの梁は1年後にはさらに輝き、その後は毎年輝きが増していくことでしょう。

こうした100年以上昔に建てられたであろう古民家が、今私たちに、人として大切なものを教えてくれるようになるのです。

土間と囲炉裏の境の部分。いよいよ完成間近の風景です。内部が仕上がると、古民家は外部の環境をも室内に反映し、大きな味わいを醸し出すようになります。室内外の空間が見事に融合する、それが古民家の大きな特徴だとおわかりいただけるように私は思います。

surrounded by the song of birds under beautiful clear skies.

It was situated in a sacred environment which can absorb all the fatigue of daily life.

This "Old folk house in the sky" was completed in 2010 and was awarded the TH Grand Prize, Reform Division, Judge's Encouragement Prize recommended by an architect, Mr. Fumio Shimizu.

When I stood at this "Old folk house in the sky", I was made to think about various things.

"Isn't it necessary to occasionally look at your life from a higher position without being buried in a noisy society?"

I was made to feel like that.

When I am staying here, I feel like I've learned something.

I had much deeper pleasure because I could receive the Judge's Encouragement Prize with this old folk house's renovation.

The right page shows the appearance of the "Old folk house in the sky" before and after renovations.

Before the renovation, wood was corroded and was damaged by white ants. Most people would look at its condition and think this building has no choice but to

be dismantled. However, my work begins with thinking about its renovation.

How can I renovate this so that the wood materials whisper, praise and start to shine? How can I heal and impress its residents? I start to explore it by thinking thoroughly.

As a result, after the renovation, the shabby old folk house was transformed into such a splendid one. It was the moment when the happy voices of the wood of the old folk house began to be heard.

Please look at this beam. The beam of several decades ago has revived. With its inhabitants and wood shining, these beams will shine even more in a year and get brighter every year.

Such old folk houses built more than 100 years ago teach us important things about being human today.

This scene is a border between the earth floor and hearth which is about to be completed. Once the interior is done, the old folk house will reflect the exterior environment in the room and bring out its enormous flavor. The air from the inside and outside merge perfectly. I think you will understand this to be a major feature of old folk houses.

事例2 150年前の「まほろばの里古民家」

次にご紹介するのは、「土佐のまほろばの里」といわれる南国市のK邸です。

115年前に当時の古材を使って建て直した再生古民家です。

この家も、持ち味のあるお家で、上手く周辺の環境を家の中に取り込んでいます。古民家が蘇ることで、古くからの史跡古墳の発掘される歴史ゆかしい香長平野周辺の空気と調和して、個性ある環境を作り出しているのです。

施工中には、昔の匠たちが心を込め、思いを込めた風格あるお家の素晴らしさが日々立ち現れました。この古民家の作りのすごさには、まさに心ときめく毎日の連続でした。

白い門柱の奥の家は、築後百数十年がたっている母屋です。門の左側は納屋となっていて、その奥の北側にある離れで施主様のご両親が住んでおられます。

少し角度を変えてみましょう。この外観は少し手を加えるだけでがらりと姿を変えてしまいます。本当に古民家の素晴らしさは底が知れません。

この古民家も、他の伝統的な農家と同じく、リフォームにリフォームを重ね、幾棟もの増改築を繰り返してきていたようです。無垢の杉板の竿ぶちの天井は、古くなったためか、今風の新建材のテックスで

150-year-old "old folk house in paradise"

This next one is the old folk house of Mr. K in the "paradise of Tosa".

The renovated old folk house was rebuilt 115 years ago with old materials.

This house also has a unique flavor bringing the surrounding environment into the house nicely. Through the renovation of the old folk house, a unique environment is created in harmony with the surrounding atmosphere of Kacho-plain where historical ruins and ancient tombs have been excavated since long ago.

During the construction, the splendor of the stately house that was heartfelt and thought out by the old craftsmen emerged daily.

I was impressed by the greatness and workmanship of this old folk house every day.

The house behind the white gatepost is a main building of more than a hundred and a few decades ago. On the left side of the gate is a barn where the parents of the owner live at a northern detached room in the back.

Let's change the angle slightly. This appearance can be completely changed by a little modification. The splendor of an old folk house is truly endless.

This old folk house has been renovated

覆い隠され、部屋の聚楽壁は、今風のプリント合板で貼り隠されていました。これでは健康に良いわけはありません。

　この合板を取り去ると、下からは本来の漆黒の梁や、柱や漆喰壁が出てきました。再生工事を完了することで、本来の素晴らしい構造が姿を現し輝き出したのです。これで、この古民家には本来の息吹がよみがえりました。想像もつかない新鮮さと、おしゃれな空間が出来上がった瞬間です。

　住まいにおいて何よりも大切なことは、そこに住まう方々の健康です。住居によって元気になり活力が湧く、そのためには希望が体の芯から湧き上がってくるような健康によい素材を使うことです。

　シンプルモダンな和と洋の融合。こうすると、和室の良さと洋室の良さのどちらも取り入れることができ、協調して共鳴させることができるようになります。これは、見学に来られたみなさんが「こんなこともできるんだ」と驚かれる古民家マジックのひとつです。

　この古民家においても大変存在感のあるキッチンダイニングとロフト。

　漆黒の大きな梁がどっしりとした安心感を醸し出しています。これらがあいまって、こころ落ち着く温かみに溢れた空間が出来上がるのです。

　玄関部分は一部増築することによって、外観が一変しました。前庭や裏庭の位置関係も環境にしっかりとマッチして、素晴らしい居住空間ができました。こうしてみると、昔の家造りはなんと奥が深いものだったのかと改めて感動してしまいます。

again and again just like other traditional farmers for the repeated extension and reconstruction of buildings. The solid cedar board and batten ceiling was covered by a modern new building material and the mud wall of the room was concealed by modern printed plywood. This is not good for your health.

When I removed the plywood, the original coal-black beam, column and gypsum wall were found beneath. By completing the renovation work, the original excellent structure appeared and started to shine. The original life of the old folk house was revived. This is the moment of accomplishing a fresh and stylish space that you can't have imagined.

The well-being of the residents is the most important thing in your residence. In order to feel more energetic and energized, you need to use healthy materials that will give you hope from the core of your body.

Fusion of simple modern Japanese and Western-styles can incorporate the advantages of both allowing them to cooperate and resonate with each other. This is one of the old folk house's magic that surprises everyone who come to see it, "You can do such a thing!"

The large coal-black beams give a sense of peace of mind. Together, they create a calm and warm atmosphere.

The exterior of the entrance was completely transformed by a partial extension. The location of the front and back gardens also closely matched the environment, creating a great living space. In this way, I am impressed once again with how profound an experience the old house construction was.

こうなんしのいちちょう
香南市野市町の H 様邸

　数々の古民家の再生を手がけてきた私は、それと同じ数ほどの
人間模様を見てきました。

　何代もの祖先が暮らしてきた古民家には、辛いことや楽しいことな
どを含めて、生きてきた思い出がいっぱいに詰まっています。

　そこにはすべてを包み込んで苦労を乗り越えてきた、温かい人たち
の心と負けなかった心の強さが染み込んでいるのです。

　そんな中から特に印象に残っている古民家を紹介しましょう。

　あれは 2009 年の冬のことでした。

　町内で開かれていたお祭りに、囲炉裏のあるリフォーム展示場を開
放していた私の元に、T さんというご年配のご婦人が一人で来られま
した。

　数年前から、娘家族のご苦労を十二分に知っていた T さんは、娘
家族の住む崩れかけた古民家の修繕と、家族の幸せの原点であるその
家を何とか快適にしてあげたいと、心を砕かれていたご様子でした。

　聞けば、130年も
前の古民家とのこと
でした。

　恐らくは、今まで
に何度もリフォーム
が繰り返されてきて
いるようでした。

　場所は高知県香南
市野市町本村、景勝

Case 3 House of Mr. H in Noichi-town, Konan-city

Having worked on the renovation of many old folk houses, I have seen the same number of human patterns. The old folk house, where many generations of ancestors have lived, is full of living memories, including painful and fun things.

It is filled with the warm hearts of warm people and the strength of their unbeatable hearts, who have wrapped up everything and overcame their hardships.

Let's introduce an old folk house, which left a particularly strong impression.

It was the winter of 2009.

An elderly lady named Ms. T came alone to me when I had opened the renovation exhibition room having a fireplace during a town festival.

For several years, it seemed that she had been eager to repair the fallen old folk house where her daughter's family lived and to make the house, the origin of family happiness, comfortable.

I heard it was an 130 years old folk house years.

It seemed that renovations had occurred repeatedly over the years.

It is located at the eastern foot of Sanpo-mountain, a scenic spot in Honmura, Noichi-town, Konan-city, in Kochi Prefecture. It was a 130-year-old house of one story, built on the hill.

It was an Irimoya (hip-and-gable roof) style house with a simple appearance and plaster-coated white walls. Traces of its excellent building reminded me of white egret and elegant cranes remained everywhere and the techniques of craftsmanship were shining.

地である三宝山の東の麓にある古民家。山裾の高台に立つ平屋建ての築後130年の民家でした。

　シンプルな外観、白壁の漆喰塗の入母屋の家です。白鷺や清楚で優雅な鶴を思わせるような名建築の痕跡が随所に残り、職人たちの匠の技が光っていました。

　旧家で門の反対側には蔵があり、門をくぐると中庭があって、崩れかけた炊事場の隣に母屋が立っていました。

　南側と東側の外観、どちらの方向からも、壮大な太平洋に面した、野市町の香長平野の素晴らしい景色が臨めます。この素晴らしい外部環境を引き込めば、この古民家はきっと地域の評判の場所になるだろうと私は大きな期待をしていました。

　そして2010年の7月、この古民家の再生工事を始めたのです。

　天井を解体してみると、荒削りの丸梁が組み合わされていました。このような梁や柱で、重い屋根瓦や赤土をしっかりと支えているのです。これら無作為の梁や桁の美しさは、見れば見るほど輝きを放ってくる不思議な魅力にあふれています。

　母屋の再生工事は、間取りも

There was a storehouse to the opposite side of the gate which was common to the ancestral family. There was a courtyard after passing through the gate and the main building was built next to a crumbling kitchen.

You can view a wonderful scenery of Noichi-town Kacho plain facing the great Pacific Ocean from both south and east sides. I had a great expectation that if I could draw this wonderful outer environment into the old folk house, it would become a place of reputation for the region.

I started the renovation of this old folk house in July 2010.

When I dismantled the ceiling, roughly shaved round beams were found to be combined. Heavy roof tiles and red soil were supported by such beams and columns. The beauty of such random beams and cross beams are full of magical charm. The more you see them the more they shine.

The room layout of the main building was made very simple for the renovation. Two tatami rooms were left in their original form

いたってシンプルなものにしました。畳部屋の二間はそのまま残して、あとはすべて洋室に変えました。

　この家のメインは、キッチンを中心にしたLDKです。そのため、南面の一番良い場所の中心にこれを持っていきました。

　特殊な断熱材を使っていますので、冷暖房も小さな容量の機器で十分に対応できます。

　さらに、別棟にあった風呂とトイレと洗面所を、家の中に組み込みました。南側の縁側もそのまま残しました。室内と外部の一体感と、素晴らしい景勝地を眺望できるようになっている点を生かさない手はないと思ったからです。

　こちらがようやく完成した邸宅です。古民家ときめき再生によって、素晴らしい内部と外部の名建築が損なわれることなく生かされ、歴史の持つ美しさと当時の匠の技が随所にみられる快適な邸宅へと生

and all the rest were changed into Western rooms.

The main part of this house is LDK centered on the kitchen. Therefore, I allocated it in the center of the best place on the south side.

Owing to special heat insulation materials, heating and cooling can be done well with a small volume equipment.

In addition, the bath, toilet and washing room in the separate building was incorporated into the house. I also left the south veranda as it was. I thought I would take advantage of its unity of inside and outside where you can view the wonderful scenic vistas.

These are the photos of the finished house. Through the "old folk house wonder renovation", it was revived as a comfortable residence where excellent architecture of inside and outside were utilized without damaging the beauty of the history and techniques of the craftsmanship.

まれ変わりました。

　雨漏りで傷んでいたために取り壊した釜屋部分には玄関を設けました。

　古い漆喰塗の雰囲気を生かして、古い土壁や瓦も無駄にせず、玄関の通路の土間に活用しています。

　ところが、このような感じで着々と作業を進め、いよいよ完成間近という頃でした。

　娘さんのご家族から、Ｔさんが亡くなったという知らせが届いたのです。

　心筋梗塞による急逝でした。

　ほんのこの間まで、私の自宅を訪ねてこられたばかりだったのに……。何かの間違いではないかと、何度も思いました。私にとっては本当にショックな出来事でした。

　この邸宅の施主さんからいただいたお言葉があります。

「亡くなった母も今日は本当に喜んでくれて、ここへ見に来てくれているだろう……。私も母に良い報告ができて本当に感謝しています」

　この伝言は建築家にとって冥利に尽きる言葉でした。私にとっては何よりもありがたいお言葉です。

　でも、一番喜んでくださったのは娘さんのご家族だったと思います。その喜びの陰には、海より深いお母さまＴさんの愛情の賜物があったのだろうと、深く感じさせられました。

　そして今もこの古民家を見るたびに、
「片岡さん、本当にありがとう。やっと私の念願がかなって、もう心残りがなくなりました」
　そんなＴさんの声が聞こえてくるように思えてなりませんでした。

A front door was set up in the kiln that was demolished because it was damaged by a leak.

Taking advantage of the atmosphere of the old plaster wall, the old clay wall and tiles were not wasted and were used in the earthen floor of the entrance passage.

When I was incessantly working on the project and getting closer to its completion, I was informed by her daughter's family that Ms. T had died of cardiac infarction.

She had just visited my house recently. It was a very shocking event for me.

I have received a message from the owner of this house.

"I felt as if my deceased mother was very happy and came to see the house today. I am really grateful for having been able to give a good report to my mother."

I've felt so lucky to receive such words as an architect. They were grateful words for me.

But I think it was the family of her daughter who was most pleased with it. I deeply felt that there was a gift of deep love from Ms. T behind the joy.

Whenever I saw the old folk house, I felt as if her voice was heard.

"Thank you, Mr. Kataoka. My wish has come true and I have no more regrets."

亡き母の思いも強き行く末の幸多かれと我が子の住み家

　こんな歌をメモに書きつけておくほど、この体験は強烈なものでした。

　このように親族、特に親の世代がきっかけで、古民家の再生工事を選択する方々が、多くなってきました。また最近では、若い女性の方が古民家を購入して再生工事をしてほしいといわれる例が増えてきているのです。

　自分の親が生活に不自由で、それを辛抱しているのを見ることほど悲しく辛いものはありません。

　両親が共に健康で、快適な毎日を送っていることは子どもたちに勇気と元気を与えてくれるものです。その源となるのが『五感を刺激する古民家』なのです。

　古い家を直したいという人は、住まいに思い入れのある方たちです。打ち合わせの段階から家族の全員が集まります。そして、特に高齢者の方は、完成した時に「まるで新しい家族ができて見守ってくれているようだ」と喜んでくださるのです。

　お話を聞いていると、ほとんどの方の目が輝き、心ときめいておられるのが、私にもひしひしと伝わってきます。

　古い物への愛着なのか、それともご自身や自分の祖先の歴史が刻まれたお住まいが、蘇ったことへの感激からなのでしょうか。

　それは、日本人に本来備わっている DNA が、かき立てられているのかもしれません。

　とにかく、お客さまのそうした心のワクワク感が伝わってきて、私の方もつい感動してしまうことがしばしばあるのです。

　例えば、これは別の出来事だったのですが、築後 43 年の古民家を

Strong wish of deceased mother

A lot of good luck in the future to my child's residence

This experience was so intense that I wrote this tanka poetry in my notes.

In this way, the number of people who have chosen to renovate old folk houses has increased, because of their relatives, especially the generation of their parents. Recently, there have been an increasing number of cases where young women purchase old folk houses and ask to do renovation work.

Nothing is more sad and painful than seeing your parents growing old and frail.

Having both parents healthy and comfortable every day gives children courage and energy. The source of this is the "old folk house that stimulates the five senses"

Those who want to renovate their old houses are those who have passion for their lives.

From the meeting stage, the whole family gets together. Elderly people are especially pleased at the time of completion. "It's like having a new family watching over me".

When I listen to the story, I can feel that most of the people's eyes are shining, and their hearts are throbbing.

Is it an attachment to the old things or is it because of the excitement that the house with their own history and their ancestors has been revived?

It may be because the DNA inherent to Japanese people has been stirred.

The excitement of the customer's heart is always transmitted, and I am often impressed.

再生後の「I様邸」LDK部分　築後43年
43-year-old "House of Ms. I" after renovation, LDK part

再生したことがありました。

　生まれ変わった改装の家に、介護施設に入院していて、家族との会話もすることができなかった車椅子のおばあちゃんが、木の香りが漂うわが家に帰ってきて、その中に入った途端、

「えいねえ！　えいねえ！」

　そう言いながら、車椅子で見て回っている母親の姿を見て、娘さん方の家族一同が感動して涙したというお手紙を頂いたこともありました。

For example, this was a different event when I'd renovated a 43-year-old house.

When a grandmother in a wheelchair who used to be hospitalized in a nursing care facility and could not even have a conversation with her family came back and entered the renovated house filled with wood scent, she uttered, "I like it! I like it!". I received a letter saying that her daughter's family were all moved to tears when they saw her mother moving around in her wheelchair.

再生前 「43 年前の I 様邸」 LDK 部分
43-year-old "House of Ms. I" before renovation, LDK portion

事例4 香南市野市町のK様邸

（THリフォーム部門大賞　地域最優秀部門賞受賞）

2009年8月に完成した、高知県香南市野市町の中ノ村にあるK様邸の話です。それは田舎の農家の豪邸でした。

敷地の中には、昔の素晴らしい面影が残っていました。

そこで現代の良さを十分に取り入れながら、建物も含めて外部空間もそのまま素直に復元をしてみると、意外な空間が出来上がりました。

暗くて寒いから使えないという部屋が多かった家が、多くの問題をすべて解決して、現代風の新築にはない、魅力ある空間に生まれ変わっていたのです。

旧家の先代から受け継がれ、思いを込められて守り継がれた150年以上もたった古民家が、再生工事で蘇ったのです。今では、家族全員に喜ばれ、快適に生活されているようです。

しかし、築後150年という平屋の民家の家と、それに併設して40年ほど前に増築した2階建ての家を再生する場合、古い家を壊して新築にするか、それとも古い家を再生するかで迷う方が多いようです。これは考えさせられる問題だと思います。

そこで覚えておいていただきたいのは、暑さや寒さを断熱材で対応し、巨大な地震に備えて現代の耐震補強工事を駆使すること、そして最新資材の活用によって、安全・安心・快適・健康のキーワードをす

Case 4 House of Mr. K in Noichi-town, Konan-city

(TH Reform section Grand Prize, Regional Best Category Award)

This is the story of the house of Mr. K in Nakanomura, Noichi-town, Konan-city, Kochi-Prefecture completed in August 2009. It was the magnificent house of a farmer in the countryside.

There was a wonderful remnant of the old days at the site.

So, while fully incorporating the best of modern times, when I tried to restore the external space including the building as it was, an unexpected space was created.

Many rooms were not accessible due to the darkness and coldness, but all the problems were solved and the house was transformed into an attractive space that can't be found in a modern new building.

Over 150-year-old folk house, which had been carefully inherited from previous generations of the old family, was revived through

べて生かすことによって、古民家は立派に再生し、新築に負けない住まいに変えることができるということです。

この香南市の古民家を再生した時に、そこの施主さんがしみじみと次のように語ってくださいました。

「新築かリフォームかで迷い、最終的に再生リフォームすると決めたときに、母が本当に喜んでくれた。先祖から受け継がれたものを新しい技術を取り入れて直し、次の代に引き継いでいくことの大切さを、その母の喜ぶ顔を見て教えてもらいました」

とても印象的な言葉でした。このお家に関して言えば、夏は風通しを良くして、エアコンなしでも十分に涼しくなるように造り替え、冬は、蓄熱式の24時間暖房を全館に取り入れて暖かくなるようにしました。それに合わせて太陽光発電を設置して、環境にも災害にも配慮した古民家住宅に再生させたのです。

古い天井を残したいというのは、この家の若奥さんの強い希望でしたので、和室も天井を中央部に残し、屋根裏の梁を全面に出しました。匠がなせる技の見せどころです。

また、欄間の透かしを生かすことによって、リビングの光がその

renovation. Today, the whole family seems to be happy and living in comfort.

However, if you are going to renovate a 150-year-old one-story private house and a two-story house that was added about 40 years ago, many tend to be confused whether to destroy the old house and build a new one or to renovate the old one. This is a serious issue to be considered.

Therefore, please keep in mind that old folk houses can be renovated splendidly and transformed into houses equal to new buildings if you can handle heat/cold with insulation, the modern seismic reinforcement work in preparation for a massive earthquake and install all equipment related to safety, security, comfort and health using the most up-to-date technology.

When I renovated this old folk house in Konan-city, the owner talked to me quietly with these words:

"My mother was really pleased when I finally decided to renovate the house after having wondered whether to build a new building or to renovate it. Looking at her happy face, I was taught the importance of incorporating new technology into what was inherited from our ancestors and passing it on to the next generation."

These were very impressive words. Speaking of this house, I renovated it so that it was cool enough without air conditioning in summer and made it warm by adding a 24-hour heat storage system in winter. Solar power generation was installed to the renovated old folk house in consideration of both the environment and disasters.

It was a strong desire of the young wife of this house to keep the old ceiling, so it was left in the center of a Japanese style room and beams in the attic were exposed at the front. It's a highlight of the

隙間を映し出します。ま
るで走馬燈のような光と
影に癒やされます。まさ
に古民家ならではの美し
い空間に生まれ変わりま
した。これは施主であ
る、ご主人の最もお気に
入りの意外な空間だそう
です。

　40年くらい前の2階建
ての建物は、土間であっ
たキッチンの部分や、和
室の寝室の部分を、無垢
材の杉や桐材をふんだん
に使って、森林浴を体感
できるような室内空間に
仕上げました。

　最後に、屋根裏に隠れ
ていた大きな丸梁が姿を
現しました。何十年もの
間、裏方としてこの家の
強度を支え続け、家族の
命や財産を守ってきたの
です。木の艶に誇らしさ
を感じるのは、きっと私だけではないと思います。
　この漆黒の大きな梁群。周辺の空間を独特な個性あるものに変えて

しまう小屋組の圧倒的な存在感は、本当に魅力的です。

　２階建て母屋の１階部分にあるダイニングキッチンの再生工事です。完成間近の写真ですが、和室控えの間の天井部分に見える百数十年の年輪を重ねた古木は、新しいものにはない独特な雰囲気と個性を放っています。
　いくら見続けても味わいがあり、飽きることがありません。

technique from a master.

Also, by making use of the openwork of the transom, the light in the living room reflects the gap. It has been transformed into a beautiful space that is unique to the old folk house. It becomes the owner's most favorite, unexpected space.

A 2 story building was finished about 40 years ago as a space where you can experience forest bathing by using plenty of solid woods, such as cedars and paulownias, in a kitchen where there used to be a dirt floor and a Japanese style bedroom.

Finally, a large round beam appeared which was hidden in the attic. It has been supporting the strength of the house and protecting family lives and assets. I'm sure I'm not the only one who feels pride in the luster of wood.

This is a renovation work of the dining kitchen on the first floor of the 2-story main building. This is the photo when it is about to be completed, but the old tree with hundreds of decades of annual rings that can be seen in the ceiling of the Japanese-style anteroom has a unique atmosphere and individuality that is not found in new ones.

No matter how much you keep watching, you will never get tired of its savor.

事例 5　西佐古の古民家

　写真は高知県香南市野市町の西佐古という場所にある古民家物件です。

　この建物は、築後60から70年くらいを経た建物ですが、新築時の時から、古材の梁や柱を使って建てられていたであろうと思われる建物です。

　昔の大工さんや、家をつくられた施主さんには、物を粗末にしないという考え方が常に底流にあったのだと痛感させられる物件です。このように昔の日本には本当に素晴らしい文化があったのだと感心し、感動するばかりです。

　外回りの外壁は、焼き杉板張りです。壁は大部分が土壁塗りになっていて、日当たりは満点。三方が道路に面していますので、大変に便利でした。

Case 5 An old folk house in Nishisako

This is the photo of an old folk house in Nishisako, Noichi-town, Konan-city, in Kochi Prefecture.

This building is a 60 to 70-year-old one originally and seems to be built by using old beams and columns.

This property made me realize that old carpenters and owners who built houses always had did so with the intent of not wasting things. As such, I am impressed and moved that Japan used to have such a wonderful culture.

The outer wall circumference is made of burnt cedar boards. Most of the walls were painted with earthen walls and the sunlight was perfect. It was very convenient because three sides face the road.

I lowered the exterior block and attached round semi-circular ridge-roof tiles and applied Tosa plaster, you will notice its drastic change of appearance just by doing this. After that, depending on the sensibility of the inhabitants, the expressions of old folk houses varies widely.

Inside the entrance, old eaves tiles were buried in the earthen floor.

Walls and ceilings were covered by Tosa Japanese paper.

Old wooden beams give an imposing presence in the living space.

There is a loft above the dining room, making use of the attic space without waste.

In the back of the photo (B), a large sun deck with roof was installed. This allows the view of the garden to be part of the room and the outside space to be merged into the room.

In the renovated old folk house in Nishisako, existence of a large round beam which has been protecting the owner and his family

この外部のブロック塀を少し低くし、棟瓦は雁振^{がんぶ}りをつけて土佐漆喰を塗りました。こうするだけで外見の表情は、ガラッと変わることに気がつかれると思います。後は住む方の感性次第で、古民家は味わいと表情が多様に変化します。

　玄関を入った内部には土間に古い軒瓦を埋め込みました。

　壁天井は土佐和紙です。古木の柱梁^{ちゅうりょう}が堂々^{どうどう}とした存在感を出しています。

　リビングの空間も、古木の柱梁を生かした造りになっています。

　ダイニングの上にはロフトがあり、屋根裏の空間を無駄^{むだ}なく活用しています。

　下の左の写真の奥には、屋根付きの広いサンデッキを付けました。こうすることで、庭の景色も部屋の一部として、また外部の空間も融合させて室内に取り込むことができるのです。

　再生された西佐古の古民家は、数十年屋根裏で、家主とその家族を

(B)

and providing safety and security for several decades in the attic creates a unique space. This is a great example of how the fusion of old and new materials has made each other's materials more attractive and has created an atmosphere that cannot be expressed in a new building.

The "Wonder (Joyful) Renovation of Traditional Japanese Old Folk House" which we've been working on is a house that has stored the thought of the old carpenters and owners who built it.

Such old folk houses have a magical power. There is no way but to otherwise. to experience. I would like to invite all of you to actually experience an old folk house.

My ideal house building is "to create a self-sufficient house".

There are many hidden essences of the ideal house in such an old building.

In old folk houses, wisdom cultivated in daily life in the long his-

守り、安全、安心を与え続けてきた大きな丸梁の存在が、独特な空間を作り上げています。古いものと新しいものの融合で、お互いの素材のよさを引き立てあい、新築では表現できない味わいを醸し出したという好例です。

この民家を創られた、昔の大工さんやお施主さんの思いをしっかりと受け止め、取り入れた家造りなのが、今、私たちが行っている古民家ときめき再生です。

こうした古民家には、不思議なパワーが存在しています。これは体感していただく以外に方法がありません。ぜひ、みなさんに実際に古民家で体感していただきたいと思うばかりです。

私の理想の家造りは、「自給自足の家を創ること」です。

理想の家の原点が、随所に隠されているのが、こうした古い建物にはあります。

古民家には、人間の長い歴史の中で、生活で培われてきた英知があらゆるところに生かされています。そうした英知を今こそしっかりと学び、受け継いでいかなければいけないと思っています。エネルギーから食料まですべて自分の敷地と建物でまかなっていくことができる家。これは、理論的にもまた現実的な技術の面でも可能な条件が近年生まれつつありますので、私たちはより高度な「自給自足の家」を目指して取り組んでいるところです。

本山町　北山山荘「ゆずハウス」の南側縁側と庭部分
Motoyama-town, Kitayama lodge
"citron house" South veranda and garden

tory of human beings is present everywhere. I think it's time to study further and reap the wisdom. A house where you can have everything, from energy to food, on your own site and building. We have been targeting the higher level "self-sufficient house" as there are solutions that have emerged recently which make it possible both theoretically and technically.

事例 6 　地産地消の古民家
（ちさんちしょう）

　高知県の杉をふんだんに使った、2 階建ての 30 坪ほどの木造住宅です。

　壁は土佐和紙や珪藻土壁。天井は杉や土佐和紙や桐板を使って、自然素材で作り上げています。こうした材料が、住む人に対して、実に優しく心地よい空間と空気を創り上げていくのです。

　2 階の寝室は、杉の床板に土佐和紙の壁と素材にこだわって作りました。

　杉とヒノキの天井で仕上げていて、屋根裏がありません。その分だけ天井が高いので気持ちのよい広い空間になりました。山小屋のような杉をふんだんに使った空間は、精神を安定させ、熟睡の効果もあるようです。まさに、人が木によって癒やされる空間の誕生といってよいでしょう。

　ところで、再生工事や木造の新築工事に携わっていると、お客さまからよくこんなことを聞かれます。

「県内産の木を使う場合、スギよりもヒノキが強いのではないのですか？」

　……確かに、単品の木材だけの強度を比べると、そのとおりです。

　しかし、家の場合は軸組みを組み合わせて構造体にするので、接合部分の金物の強度に準じた強さを発揮することには、ヒノキであろうとスギであろうと、同じだという結果が出ています。

An old folk house, local production for local consumption

This is a 2-story wooden house about 100 square meter in size, using abundant cedar, in Kochi Prefecture. It was made from natural materials such as Tosa Japanese paper, diatom mud for the walls and cedar. Tosa Japanese paper and paulownia board for the ceiling. Such materials are creating a truly gentle, spacious and comfortable space for the residents.

The bedroom on the second floor is made with specific materials such as cedar floor boards and Tosa Japanese paper walls.

There is no attic because it is finished with a cedar and cypress ceiling. Therefore, it became a pleasant and spacious large room due to its higher walls. A space using abundant cedar like a mountain lodge stabilizes your mind and helps you sleep well. It can be

少し専門的になって分かりにくいかもしれませんが、構造体にすると、強度が何倍も大きくなり、それに伴う接合金物が必要になって、それがバランスを保つのです。

　例えば、同じ紙でも、折り曲げたり、組み合わせたりすることで、その強さが変わってきます。

　構造体にすると、折り紙であっても、橋にして、なおその上に携帯電話を載せても支えることができる強度になります。折り紙単体だけだと、あっという間にバラバラになってしまいます。同じことが建築物、木材の梁についても言えるわけです。

　その後は、それぞれの木材に合った工夫をすることで、材質に関係なく安全な使用が可能です。それでもあえて木材の質にこだわるなら、私たちの健康や元気を維持していくための効用や効能、あるいは触感や匂いなどの好みで樹種を決めるのがよいでしょう。

　さて、2階の子ども部屋です。撮影当時はまだ完成していませんでしたが、上部の奥にロフトを作りました。

　子ども部屋から両サイドに梯子を掛けて、上がり下りするようになります。

　ロフトの北の窓を開けると、気持ちのよい風が通り抜けていきます。

　ここにも天井裏がありませんが、特殊な断熱材を使うことで快適な空間となっています。

said that it is the birth of a space where people are healed by trees.

By the way, customers often ask me the following as I am engaged in renovation work and new wooden construction.

"When using trees from the prefecture, isn't the cypress stronger than the cedar?"

Actually, if you compare the strength of a single piece of wood, that is right.

However, in the case of a house, the shaft assembly is combined to form a structure, so the strength of the metal and wood at the junction is almost the same whether it is a cypress or a cedar.

It may be a bit technical and difficult to understand, but when it comes to structure, the strength is many times higher, and the accompanying joint metal is needed to keep the balance.

If there is a structure, it will be strong enough to support something even if it is made of origami paper. If the paper is made into a bridge, a mobile phone can be placed on it. If it's just a piece of origami paper, it doesn't work. The same is true for buildings and timber beams.

Following that, by using appropriate techniques for each type of wood, it is possible to use the wood safely regardless of the material. But if you are still concerned about the quality of the wood, you can choose the species based on its utility or efficacy to keep you healthy, or your favorite taste or smell, etc.

Let's have a look at the kid's room on the second floor. I made a loft at the back after taking the photo.

You can climb up and down by a ladder on both sides of the kid's room.

There is no attic either but it's a comfortable space due to special insulation material.

事例7 古民家再生は地域を越えて 『淡路島(あわじしま)の古民家』

　高知県を飛び越えて、隣の徳島県を越えた兵庫県淡路島で「古民家ときめき再生」物件が誕生しました。私にとっては、県外第一号の古民家ときめきの再生物件でした。

　新しい古民家の誕生に、心をときめかせながら建設させていただきました。

　再生前の玄関は、主を失ってどれくらいの月日が流れたのかと感慨深い(かんがいぶか)姿だったのです。

　この物件は、基礎にも切り石を見事に組み合わせた、手の込んだ造りとなっていました。

　窓の格子戸(こうしど)にも、奥深い匠の技術と日本の伝統文化が垣間見(かいまみ)られて感動しました。

　これは、ただただ「すごい」としか言いようがありません。この古民家を見に行った時に、私は大変勉強させてもらった感謝の気持ちでいっぱいになりました。

　昔の面影が、そのまま残っている井戸と石造りの洗い場は、その当時の生活風情(ふぜい)が目に映るようでした。不便さの中にこそ、人とのコミュニケーションが必然的に生まれたのでしょう。

　100年を越した古民家によくある、太い梁もみせてもらいました。

　築百年を超える古民家は、そのほとんどが写真のように屋根瓦の下

Renovation of old folk house beyond my own region "An old folk house in Awaji-island"

A property by "Wonder (Joyful) Renovation of Traditional Japanese Old Folk House" was born in Awaji-island, Hyogo Prefecture, beyond Kochi Prefecture and neighboring Tokushima Prefecture. It was the first case of renovation outside of Kochi Prefecture for me.

I was thrilled to build the new old folk house.

The front porch before the renovation had a very emotional appearance, which made me feel how long had passed since the loss of the lord.

This property was built in an elaborate style, with a fine combination of cut stones as its foundation.

I was moved by the profound techniques of the craftsmen and Japanese traditional culture present in the lattice door of the window. This is just amazing. When I visited to see this old folk house, I was filled with gratitude for the deep opportunity to study it.

The well and the stone wash area, which still retain the old features, seemed to reflect the lifestyle of the time. Communication among people was inevitably created due to the inconvenience.

I was shown the thick beams that are common in the hundred-year-old house.

の野地板（のじいた）が竹でつくられています。その竹が100年以上も経過しているのに、全くと言っていいほど傷んでないのは驚くべき技術です。まさに古民家の英知と呼べるものです。

　今回は『廃材をできるだけ少なくして、できる限り有効利用した再生を行う』というテーマを掲げて再生工事に取り組みました。その結果は今までになくすごいものでした。2tトラック1台分の廃材（新建材）処分で済み、古木の廃材を利用することでかえってそれが魅力になったのです。

　この淡路島のお家が「古民家ときめき再生」でどのように蘇った

のか、ご覧いただいている写真だけでは、この心地よさは伝わらないかもしれません。

　再生古民家がいかに心地よいか、当社の再生古民家を見学していただいて実感（じっかん）してほしいと思うばかりです。

Most of the over 100-year-old houses' roofing boards are made of bamboo under the roof tiles, as shown in the photo. It is a testament to the amazing technique that the bamboo has not been damaged over 100 years. This is indeed is the wisdom of the old folk house.

On this occasion, I did the renovation with the theme "reduce and recycle waste wood as much as possible". The result was more amazing than ever. There was only a two-ton truck of waste material (new building materials) and our reuse of the old wood waste material made it more attractive.

These photos may not be sufficient to show you how the comfort of this house in Awaji-island was revived.

I just want you to visit our renovated old folk house and realize how comfortable it is.

私の
「古民家ときめき再生」哲学

My philosophy on "Wonder renovation of old folk houses"

私は木の温もりに包まれ、自然に抱かれたような感覚を与えてくれる木造建築こそが、日本人に最もふさわしい建築だと思っています。

　一家が三世代にわたり、コミュニケーションを交わしながら、木の温もりに包まれて、お互いを気遣い合い、励まし合って暮らす伝統的な文化が、日本の民家には本然的（ほんぜんてき）に備わっています。人間は自然によって感化され、癒やされ、充電することができる。そこに人の優しさが蘇ってきます。木にはそうした、自然の不思議な、大きなパワーが潜（ひそ）んでいます。

　私は日頃から、木そのもののもつ素晴らしさを感じて建築に携わっていますが、それは「古民家ときめき再生」事業でも変わることはありません。むしろ古い民家だからこそ、木の持つ宝のようなパワーを感じずにはいられないのです。

　これらの思いの中で、どの家の再生にも生かし続ける五つの古民家再生の哲学を持っています。私がもっとも大切にしている哲学とともに、どのように「古民家ときめき再生」に取り組んでいるかを紹介したいと思います。

再生後の「佐川町Ｈ様邸」築後 120 年
120-year-old "House of Mr. H in Sagawa-town" after renovation

I believe that the most suitable architecture for the Japanese is the wooden architecture, which is wrapped in the warmth of wood and gives a feeling of being embraced naturally.

再生後の「K 様邸」南面 築後 150 年以上
Over 150-year-old "House of Mr. K" south side

Japanese private houses have a traditional culture of living in the warmth of wood, caring for each other, and encouraging each other while communicating with each other among three generations. Human beings can be inspired, healed and recharged by nature. The

再生後の「K 様邸」LDK 室内 築後 35 年以上
Over 35-year-old "House of Mr. K" after renovation, LDK

kindness of people is revived within such houses. Trees store the mysterious power of nature.

I've been involved with architecture through feeling the splendor of the tree itself usually. It is even more the case in "Wonder Renovation of Old Folk Houses" project. Because it is an old private house, I cannot help feeling the power of a tree like a treasure.

In this way, I have five philosophies for renovating old folk houses which I apply for the revival of any house. I would like to introduce to you how we're working on the "Wonder Renovation of Old Folk Houses" along with the philosophies I value most.

哲学 1 住む方の声を聞く

どの古民家再生でも、そこに住まわれているご家族のことを何より
も大切に考えて施工することが大切です。そのためには、現在そこに
ある古い建築物と新しい技術を融合させることが最も重要になってき
ます。

古民家再生というと、よく勘違いをされるのが「昔そのままの家を
復元をするのではないか」と思われる人もいますが、それは全くの誤
解です。

私が進めている「古民家ときめき再生」とは、今までの建築におけ
る新築やリフォームや増改築工事とは、全く違った工事形態なのです。

新築や増改築は、何もないところから物事をつくっていきます。

またリフォーム工事も、建築全般の部分的なところは、見え掛かり
部分の模様替えといった、表面上の直しといった側面（そくめん）が強く、どちら
かというと、できるだけ新築に近づけようという工事手法です。

しかし、私どもが行っている「古民家ときめき再生」は、古民家の
持つ温かさや、人間の心を癒やす心地よさを生かしながら、新しい匠
の技と新しい材料を組み合わせて、快適な居住性（きょじゅうせい）を生み出していく、
全く新しい建築手法なのです。

そのため再生工事はまず、古民家のあるがままの姿の良い部分と、
悪い部分とをしっかり調査をすることから始まります。

建物本体はもちろんのこと、使い勝手や風の通り道、環境面、快適
性、外部空間や自然環境を取り入れ、景観にマッチした建物かどうか
を考えて建てていきます。

「古民家ときめき再生」は、新たに創るというよりも、その家の個
性を磨（みが）きあげ、欠点を取り除いて、現在の技術力と新素材の活用に

Listening to the voices of the residents

When renovating an old folk house, it is important to consider the family living there above all else. To that end, it is of utmost importance to combine the old buildings that are currently there with new technologies.

When it comes to renovating old folk houses, it is often misunderstood that "the old house will be restored." However, it is a complete misunderstanding.

"Wonder Renovation of Old Folk Houses" which I'm promoting is a completely different type of construction than the existing construction of new buildings and remodeling.

As for new buildings and remodeling, we will create things from nothing.

再生後の「芸西の古民家」築後 70 年
70-year-old "Old folk house in Geisei village" after renovation

再生後の「天空の古民家」土間南側部分
"Old folk house in the sky" after renovation, southern side of earthen floor

第3章　私の「古民家ときめき再生」哲学

In addition, a part of the remodeling work of the whole building has a strong aspect of surface repair, such as the rearrangement of the visible parts. So, it is a construction method that tries to be as close to a new construction as possible.

However, our "Wonder Renovation of Old Folk Houses" combines the new skills of masters with new materials, while taking advantage of the warmth of old folk houses and the comfort of soothing human mind. It's a whole new way of building which creates a comfortable living.

Therefore, renovation work begins by thoroughly investigating the good and bad portions of old folk houses.

By incorporating not only the building itself, but also its usability, wind path, environment, comfort, external space and natural environment, we're going to build a building that matches the landscape.

"Wonder Renovation of Old Folk Houses" is a new construction method of creating new space by brushing up an individuality of the house and removing defects and utilizing modern technology and new materials.

Renovation and remodeling of old folk houses resonates with the sensibility of the people who live and have attachment to creativity, cherishing things from the culture and traditions of Japan. The voices of the wood would then be conveyed to the heart of its residents. The more you live in an old folk house, the more it matches the sensibility of its residents. Its mysterious existence like that of a creature.

The fusion of the new and the old creates a unique charm and splendor, and when the sensibility of its inhabitants is combined with this, a more exquisite space emerges. This is exactly the magic of an old folk house.

よって、新しい空間を作り出すという新たな建築の手法なのです。

　古民家再生リフォームは、住む方と作る方との感性、愛着心、物を大切にする心、日本の文化と伝統を、共鳴させて創り上げるものです。そうすると木々たちの声が住まう人の心に伝わってくるようになるでしょう。古民家は住めば住むほど、住む人間の感性とマッチングする、生き物のような不思議な存在なのです。

　新しいものと古いものとの融合によって、そのどちらにもない魅力と素晴らしさを生み出して、住む人の感性がこれに結びつくと、さらに絶妙な空間が出現する。これはまさに古民家のマジックです。

「古い家をいじると、かえってお金がかかる。新しく作り変えた方が、家も強くなるから有利だ」

　という意見もありますが、私はその意見には疑問を抱いています。

　まず、「古民家ときめき再生」の工法は、現にあるものを十分に生かして造っていきますから、今までの施主の方々が、異口同音に言われていますが、予想以上に魅力的な古民家を予算に合わせて段階的に創り上げることが可能になります。わが家を自分流に創り上げていくという言葉がぴったりそれを表しています。

　今後古民家の貴重さ、素晴らしさはますますクローズアップされていくことでしょう。古民家の良さを再認識する時代が必ずやってきます。それはもう時間の問題だと私は思うのです。

　また技術や科学、医療が進み、木の強さや効果など、他の建材にはない良さが解明されてきています。古民家再生に携わる私から見れば、これまでの意見は間違っていると言わざるを得ません。

"If you work on an old house, it will cost you more money. It is more advantageous to make a new one, because the house will be stronger."

Although there is an opinion as above, I have doubts about it.

Our construction method utilizes existing materials fully which makes it possible to create more attractive old folk houses than expected within the budgets of the owners, and step-by-step. The words, "creating our own home in our own way" expresses it perfectly.

In the future, the preciousness and splendor of old folk houses will be more and more valued. The era of reaffirming the goodness of old folk houses will surely come. I think it's just a matter of time.

In addition, with the advancement of technology, science, and medical care, the strength and effects of wood, which are not found in other building materials, have been revealed. From my perspective, having been involved in the renovation of old folk houses, I have to say opinions so far are wrong.

哲 学

2　良質素材にこだわる

　私が行っている古民家再生は「住まいの原点とは何か？」という、人間にとって大切なテーマを追求することでもあります。今も勉強中の身ですが、現時点で私が出した結論は「自然素材」に徹する家づくりです。

　内装資材はすべて自然素材を使う。これを実行すると、入居後の居

住環境が以前とは比較にならないぐらいに快適になるのです。そして快適になればなるほど、今度はその居住環境に愛着が湧いてきます。

　例えば、珪藻土や漆喰仕上げの土壁と土佐の無垢の杉材の部屋の心地よさは素晴らしいものです。これはすべて自然素材ですから、健康にもとてもいい環境になります。

　また「断熱材」も健康的な住居をつくる上で非常に大切な役割を果たします。天井で一番重要なのは断熱材です。断熱材の素材を何にするかで、住む人の健康・快適性・省エネ・安全性が決まります。

　われわれ建築家は断熱材に、もっと神経を使う必要があります。それは高度な断熱処理は、快適性を左右する大切な部分なのです。

Focusing on high quality materials

The renovation of old folk houses that I am doing is also pursuing an important theme for human beings, "What is the origin of a res‐ idence?" I am still studying, but my conclusion at this point is to build a house that is fully committed to "natural materials".

All interior materials are made from natural materials. This will make your living environment much more comfortable after you've moved in than it used to be. And the more comfortable you become, the more you become attached to your living environment.

For example, the comfort of a room made of diatom earth or plas‐ ter walls and Tosa's solid cedar wood is wonderful. Since these are whole natural materials, it's also a much better environment for your health.

In addition, "insulation" plays a very important role in creating a healthy house. The insulating material is the most important thing about the ceiling. Selection of the heat insulating material determines the health, comfort, energy saving and safety of the resident.

We architects must pay more attention to heat insulating mate‐ rials. Advanced insulating treatment is an important part of the comfort.

Especially if the roof is not properly heat‐insulated, it will be hot in the summer and cold in winter. It will be a house where heating and cooling do not work. The true role of insulation is to reduce en‐ ergy consumption and energy costs while also merging indoor and external spaces. In other words, it is to make full use of the home's location environment by bringing in external spaces into the room.

If you are a "master of residence", you know these things. Includ‐

自然素材を使うと、この様に壁の塗りにムラができても自分流の住まいの手作りの味わいが生まれます。
The use of natural materials creates the handmade flavor of a home in one's own way, even if the paint on the walls is uneven, as shown here.

特に屋根部分の遮熱断熱処理を誤ると、夏は暑くて冬は底冷えがする。冷暖房が効きにくい住まいになります。断熱材の真の役割はエネルギー消費をできるだけ少なくして光熱費を抑え、なおかつ、室内と外部空間を融合すること。つまり、外部空間の室内への取り込みをして、家の立地環境を十二分に生かすことなのです。

　これらのことは「住の匠」であるなら、もちろん心得ているでしょう。そのことも含めて、深い経験を持つ『匠の技』は、古民家再生の重要なカギといえます。古民家再生には匠の技が絶対に不可欠です。もちろん新築物件でも匠の技の大切なことは言うまでもありませんが、古民家再生ではそれがより強く求められます。

　この匠の技の出来次第で、出来上がりの効果が大きく変わってきます。それは創り手の感性と匠の技、そして住まう側の要求によって作り上げられていくのです。

　さて、私は古民家の再生は、古いものを単に復元するのではなく、古き良きものと最新の技術力、新素材を融合して新たな価値を作り出すことだと書きましたが、それが最も端的にお見せできるのがお風呂場のような水回りについてです。

　お風呂場をユニットバス等最新式の水回りに配慮した機器にすることで、腐食やシロアリの巣となることを防ぎます。何といっても、すごく快適になり冬はヒートショックを防ぎ暖かくなるのです。

　古民家再生においては最も大切な部分であるその他の水回りにも新技術を駆使します。

　洗面やトイレなどの水回りを快適に作り変えることによって、古い民家も元気な家に変わっていきます。古いものと新しいものが見事にマッチする古民家ならではの創造です。

　例えば、洗面台と洗濯機、そして脱衣室の空間は古木の梁が見事に

ing this, the "craftsmanship" with a deep experience is an important key to the renovation of old folk houses.

By using natural materials, the hand-made taste of your personalized residence is created in spite of uneven wall paintings like this.

The technique of a master is indispensable to renovation of old folk houses. Of course, it goes without saying that craftsmanship is important even in newly built properties, but it is even more strongly required in the renovation of old folk houses. Depending on the skill of the masters, the result will vary greatly. The outcome is created through the sensibility of the architect, the skill of the craftsman, and the demands of the inhabitants.

Now, I've written that the renovation of old folk houses is not just the restoration of old things, but the fusion of good old things with the latest technology and new materials, to create new value. The

調和して味わい深い空間を創り上げます。

　そしてトイレは最もきれいに、そして清潔にしておく必要のある場所です。ここは古い木の梁や柱の空間と、最新式の水回りの商品という、異なった二つの品物を組み合わせることによって、双方の良さを互いに引き立て合う空間ができるのです。

　古い建物の短所として嫌われる『暗い』『寒い』『埃っぽい』『古臭い』『泥臭い、垢が抜けない』等々、どちらかというと短所や、欠点のほうを指摘する声が多くありました。

　ですが、こういった古民家の悩みの種の解決の秘訣はズバリ、暗く陰気な部分に新技術を取り入れて「明るくする」ことなのです。

simplest example I can show you is a water space, such as a bathroom.

By making the bathroom with state-of-the-art water-friendly devices such as a unit bath, it is possible to prevent corrosion and white ant nests. After all, it becomes very comfortable and prevents heat shock and stays warmer in winter.

We will make use of new technology for other water spaces which is the most important part of old folk houses' renovation. By remodeling the water equipment, such as washbasins and toilets, old private houses will turn into healthy houses. It is a creation unique to old folk houses where old and new things match in harmony.

For example, the space with wash basin, washing machine and dressing room creates a tasteful space where the old wooden beams are in perfect harmony.

And the toilet is a place that needs to be most clean and kept clean. By combining these two different items: the old wooden beam and the column space with state-of-the-art water equipment, it will create a space that complements the goodness of both sides.

Many people have pointed out the disadvantages of old buildings, such as "dark", "cold", "dusty", "old-fashioned", "muddy smell and rustic", etc.

However, the solutions for such troubles in old folk houses are to introduce new technology and make them "bright".

哲学 3　風の通り道をつくる

　ここで紹介するのは先ほどの「まほろばの里の古民家」です。

　現在は気持ちのいい、風の通る和室二間続きで、この北側に洋間の寝室があります。

　しかし、あちこちに放置された古い民家は、風が通らないために様々な問題が起きています。

　人が住まなくなり、空き家のままで締め切られた古民家は、風の通りがなくなるために、湿度調節ができなくなり、カビの発生や腐食、蟻害の温床となって、木の寿命を一気に縮めてしまいます。

　ですから、もし古い民家をお持ちになっているなら、住んでいなくてもときどき風を通しておくことが大切です。

　また、古民家ときめき再生では、家と外部の接点としての風の通り道を第一に考え、生かしていくことを大切にしています。

　今までにも何度も書いてきましたが、古民家は外の環境と室内の環境を融合し、取り込んで、その空気感に表現することのできない「古民家マジック」ともいえる不思議な効果を持っています。

Philosophy 3 · Creating wind passages

I would like to introduce "old folk house in paradise" from before.

There are two comfortable and ventilated Japanese-style rooms and there is a Western-style bedroom on the north side.

However, there are various problems due to a lack of airstream inside old houses remaining in various places.

Old folk houses that are closed due to the lack of people will not be able to control the humidity due to the lack of

再生後の「天空の古民家」リビング部分
"Old folk house in paradise" after renovation, Japanese room

wind passage, and will become a hotbed for mold growth, corrosion, and ant damage, shortening the life of the tree at once.

Therefore, if you have an old private house, it's important to ventilate from time to time even if you are not living in it.

風の抜ける道を作る。そのことが、古民家にさらなる新しい息吹を与えることになるのです。

　風の通り道に咲く草花は、周辺の空間の気をさわやかに一変させるのと同じです。

　その空間が活力と癒やしの場所に変わるのです。

再生後の「まほろばの里古民家」和室部分
"Old folk house in the sky" Living room

In the 'Wonder renovation of old folk houses', it is important to take advantage of the wind passages as an interface between the house and the outside.

As I have written many times before, old folk houses have a mysterious effect that can be called "old folk house magic" that cannot be expressed in the atmosphere by fusing and incorporating the outside environment and the indoor environment.

It is the same as flowers blooming in the path of the wind that refreshingly change the atmosphere of the surrounding area.

The space turns into a place of vitality and healing.

4 梁の声を聞く

哲学

この表題についてお話しするためには、私が古民家について日頃から思っていることを語る必要がありそうです。

どの古民家にも、その家の独特な空気感が漂っています。その空気感は、私たちの五感に働きかけてきて、不思議な感覚にしてくれます。まるで幼少期(ようしょうき)に、母親に抱かれているような……。

あるいは、おばあちゃんの膝枕(ひざまくら)で日向(ひなた)ぼっこをしているような……。

そんな安心感と優しさに包まれていると、何か大切なものを、ふと思い起こすことができるのです。

そういう意味で、古民家の中はまるで異空間です。

時間が止まり、かつての幼かった日々にまで、心を一気に引き戻してくれる。そして、私たちの心の中に、そっと囁(ささや)きかけてくるのです。「大切な宝物が、目の前にいっぱいあるよ――」

以前にこの言葉を証明するかのような体験をしました。

古民家からは思いがけない物が、ひょっこりと顔を出すことがあります。

高知県の佐川町にある、おそらく100年以上も前に建てられた古民家を解体した時のことです。なんと、真剣の日本刀が2本も出てきたことがありました。

恐る恐るそっと、鞘(さや)から刀を抜き出してみましたが、見事に鍛(きた)えられて、透き通るようなシルバーグレーの、研(と)ぎ澄(す)まされたその刀身(とうしん)に、思わず吸い込まれそうになったものです。

一方、仕事をしていて、老朽化(ろうきゅうか)と風雨(ふうう)による劣化で、ボロボロになってしまった古民家の姿に出くわすと、古民家の悲しい叫びが聞こ

Listening to the voices of the beams

In order to discuss this title, I think I need to talk about what I usually think about old folk houses.

Every old folk house has its own unique atmosphere. The feeling of the air influences our five senses and makes us feel mysterious as if we were embraced by our mother in our childhood.

Or, as if we were basking in the sun on grandma's lap.

We can suddenly remember something important when we are surrounded by such a sense of safety and kindness.

In that sense, the interior of old folk houses is a completely different space.

Time ceases and brings our heart back to the days of childhood at once and whisper to us gently, "There are many precious treasures right in front of you."

I've had the experience of proving these words trued before.

Unexpected things from an old folk house may come out from time to time.

It was when I dismantled an old folk house, which was probably built over 100 years ago in Sakawa-town, Kochi Prefecture, two real Japanese swords came out.

I cautiously pulled the sword out of the sheath. It was beautifully forged. I was enchanted by the transparent silver-gray sharpened body of the sword.

On the other hand, when I encounter through my work an old folk house which was totally deteriorated by aging and wind/rain, I'm having a hard time hearing the sad cry of the old folk house.

My sad heart resonates with the cry itself. It sounds like an old

再生後の「芸西村の古民家」キッチン部分
"Old folk house in Geisei village" after renovation,
kitchen space

えてくるようでつらくなります。

その叫びはそのまま、私の心が悲しく共鳴してしまうのです。それはまるで、古民家が私に助けを求めているように聞こえて仕方がないのです。

よく考えてみると、私たちの周囲は新しいものばかりに囲まれています。結果として、古いものは、どんどん壊され、処分されてしまっているのです。

これは、人間の営みというものを集約した、英知や記録そのものを、抹殺している行為ではないかと考えこんでしまいます。

言いかえれば、年老いて働くことができなくなれば、人間も物と同じように粗末に扱われていくという、何ともおかしな宿命から抜け出すことができない。そんな人間の悲哀にも似た道を、同じように歩んでいっているようにも思えるのです。

『古民家と人間のお年寄り』どこか似通っているように思えてならないのです。

古民家にも、耐震補強工事などを行えば、新しい新築の建物と、全く変わらない強さを発揮します。

むしろ、新築の建物以上に、木材そのものは2割から3割ほどに強度が増して、さらに、金物を使わない木組みで構造体を組み上げるの

folk house is asking me for help.

If you think for a moment, we are surrounded by new things mainly. As a result, old things have been dismantled and disposed of one after another.

I think that this is an act of killing the wisdom and records accumulated through human activities.

In other words, if you get old and are unable to work, you cannot get out of the strange fate of being treated as poorly as things. It seems that they are walking along a similar path of human sorrow.

"Old folk houses and elderly people" I can't stop feeling as if they look alike in some ways.

If you perform seismic reinforcement works on an old folk house, it will have the same strength as a new building.

If you compare the long term strength of a hundred year old

再生後の「佐川町の古民家」リビング部分
"Old folk house in Sakawa-town" after renovation, living room

で、100年単位という長期間にわたって強さを比べてみると、圧倒的に古民家が新築よりも強いのです。

木は切り倒されてから200年から300年までの間は、強さや剛性がじわじわと2割から3割も上昇するというのですからそのように考えてよいでしょう。

先進国のヨーロッパの国々では、新しいものよりも、古い建物の方が、その価値が高く、300年前から400年前の建物が、今も大切に扱われています。

そうした古い建物の屋根の部分は、ほとんどが数百年ほど経過した木造建築でできています。

大変に皮肉なことですが、海外の人たちによって評価されると、何となく間違っていないなという気になりませんか。

今こそ日本人も、古いものをじっくりと見直して、お年寄りを大切にできる、そんな最高の文化を取り戻して、改めて創り上げる時期を迎えているのではないでしょうか。

人間が幸せに生きていくためには、利便性や快適性だけでは、いずれは行き詰まってしまうでしょう。そこには必ず、精神性が必要になってくるのです。

building, an old folk house is overwhelmingly stronger than a new building since the wood itself increases in strength by 20 to 30 percent more than a new building and the structure is assembled through its wood frame without the use of metal.

I think you can appreciate the strength and rigidity of the wood that increases gradually by 20 to 30 percent, over 200 to 300 years since they have been cut down.

In the advanced European countries, older buildings are more valuable than newer ones, and buildings from 200 to 400 years old are still being treated well.

The roofs of such old buildings are mostly made of wood in buildings that are over a few hundred years old.

It's very ironic, but when we see how foreigners value old buildings, don't you feel like we're wrong?

Now is the time for Japanese people to carefully appreciate old things, and to regain such a great culture that can cherish the aged, and recreate it.

In order to live happily, convenience and comfort alone will eventually lead to a deadlock. There will always be a need for spirituality.

古民家には、その精神性がギッシリと詰まっています。その神髄は梁です。

　例えば、この圧倒的な梁の力強さを見てください。

　天井裏に隠れていた、ススで真っ黒になってすごい存在感を出している梁です。

　この迫力！　実際に見て確かめると、本当に素晴らしいものです。

　洋室であれ、和室であれ、それぞれの良さを引き出しつつ、自らの個性を存分に出している古い梁、何度観ても見続けていても、決して飽きることはありません。

　私は梁を見た瞬間に、その家の新しく生まれ変わった姿が頭の中に浮かびます。

　普段は隠されていて人目に触れない「梁」の存在についていえば、同じ屋根裏の構造体は存在せず、それぞれの家に個性があり、独特の魅力があるということは第１章でもお話したとおりですが、まさに時代を経てますます輝く梁の迫力は見るものを圧倒します。

　先ほど触れましたが、古民家解体の際に、あの２本の日本刀が出てきた、佐川町の古民家がありましたね。

　その梁の豪快な曲線美と漆黒の太い丸梁は、まさに「あっ！」と息を飲むほど立派でした。

　この漆黒の曲線を描いた太い梁は見事です。

　こうした古材の梁や柱が、あちらこちらに造られている古民家再生物件の、新たな柱や梁となって蘇り、多くの方々の癒やしの対象となって、人々に幸せを提供していくのです。

Old folk houses are filled with such spirituality. Its soul is its beam.

For example, look at these overwhelmingly strong beams.

They are sooty black beams hidden in the ceiling and have a great presence.

How powerful they are!! It's really amazing if you actually see them.

Whether they are Western-style rooms or Japanese-style rooms, old beams can express their individuality to the fullest while drawing out their own goodness. You'll never get tired of watching them again and again.

Once I see a beam, I can visualize the image of the newly revived house in my mind.

Speaking of the existence of "beams" usually hidden and unexposed, they have unique charm according to each house's individuality whose attic structure is never identical as I discussed earlier in Chapter 1. The dynamism of the ever-shining beams is overwhelming over time.

Do you remember the old folk house in Sakawa-town where I briefly mentioned the Japanese swords were found at the time of dismantling?

The dynamic curved beauty of the beam and the charcoal-black round beams are just breathtakingly splendid.

The design of the thick charcoal-black curved beam is a work of art.

Such old beams and columns are revived as new columns and beams of renovated properties here and there, become means of healing and provide happiness to people.

哲学 5　家に活力を入れる

　古民家における光と影の演出。これは、私ども空間を演出し、住まう人々に癒やしと安心感を与える空間づくりをする者にとっては大変必要なものです。

　同じ空間でも、光と影をうまく使い分ければ、多種多様な雰囲気に空間が変化していきます。

　その変化を、住む人間の気持ちの変化に合わせて変えてみたり、また反対に、光と影を巧みに使い分けることで、住む人間の気持ちをリラックスさせてみたりと、メンタルな部分の大きな力となっていくのです。

　古民家は、光と影の演出によって、その魅力やパワーが、何倍にも膨れ上がります。

　また、先ほど述べた色鮮やかな原色も、古民家を引き立てる不思議な力を持っています。

　古民家の再生は、住まい手の感性で大きく空間を変化させていきます。住まい手の古民家を愛する「気」と呼ぶべきものが、建物に染み込んでいくからなのでしょうか。

　家づくりに何よりも大切なことは、住む人の健康です。住まうほど

Revitalizing the house

Direction of light and shadow in an old folk house. It is very important for those who create these spaces to provide a sense of healing and security to the residents.

Even within the same space, if you use light and shadow properly, the space will change in a wide variety of atmospheres.

It will become a mentally big power to see them changing according to the residents' feelings or by using light and shadow wisely to relax the residents' feelings.

The charm and power of an old folk house can be multiplied by the direction of light and shadow.

In addition, the vivid primary colors I mentioned earlier also have a mysterious power to enhance old folk houses. The renovation of old folk houses will greatly change the space depending on the sensibilities of the residents. The energy of the residents who love old folk houses are absorbed by the building.

The most important thing for a house building is the health of its residents. We must build old folk houses where residents become healthier and energetic as they live. We must aim for a renovation in which hope springs from the core of the body.

The absolute healing power that old folk houses brings to the inhabitants certainly exists.

It's just like being embraced by a mother, it's such a strong kindness. If I try to imitate this healing space with new building materials, I will never be able to create that atmosphere.

Old buildings are full of wisdom from thousands of years of our ancestors.

The culture and tradition of valuing things is directly linked to

元気になり活力が湧く、そんな古民家を作らねばなりません。希望が体の芯から湧き上がるような再生を目指さなくてはなりません。

古民家が住む人にもたらす絶対的な癒やしの力は、確実に存在しています。

それは例えて言うならば、ちょうど、母親の懐に抱かれているような、そんな強烈な優しさなのです。この癒やしの空間を、新築の建材でまねをしようと思っても、その雰囲気は絶対に出せないと思います。

古い建物には、数千年にわたる先人からの知恵が、たくさん詰まっています。

モノを大切にするという文化や伝統などは、今日のエコロジー関連の事柄や、省エネルギーといったキーワードに、そのまま結び付いています。

茅葺き屋根の古民家建築。これひとつをとっても、そこからたくさんのことを学び、教えられることに気づきます。

築後170年以上前の茅葺き屋根の古民家と今風のバンガローを併設した造りの本山町の北山山荘では、古い文化と新しい建物を融合させ、それらを家づくりに生かしていることがわかります。

周辺に広がる四季折々の自然も住環境の大切な要素です。

春になると桜が咲き誇り、夏になれば、近くにある清流で泳ぎ、アユ釣りやキャンプができます。秋は紅葉狩り、そして冬はロマンチックな雪景色へと変化する。山の良さを生かし、それを家づくりに反映

today's ecology-related issues and to concepts such as energy conservation.

This is an old folk house with a thatched-roofed. I realizes that I could learn a lot from this one.

You will see that this Kitayama mountain lodge, in Motoyama-town, with a more than 170-year-old thatched-roofed old folk house and a modern bungalow, have merged old culture with a new

再生後の「浜改田の家」築後 60 年
60-year-old "House of Hamakaida" after renovation

本山町 ゆずハウス かや葺き棟 築後 170 年以上
Over 170-year-old lemon house in Motoyama-town,
thatched building,

させることで、四季さえも、人間の感性と情緒(じょうちょ)を育てる大切な要素に変わっていくことがわかります。

私の名刺の裏にはこれらの哲学に基づいた「6つの研究課題」を書き込んであります。

【6つの研究課題】

● わが町・わが村を見直(みなお)そう

● 古きものを見直そう

● 自然環境を生かそう

● 新たなものを見据(みす)えよう

● 特技を生かそう

● 心を見直そう

　匠たちの技が残る古民家でも、古くなったという理由だけで取り壊され、消える運命にあるのは日本人の財産の大きな損失ではないでしょうか。この宝物を、私たちは何としても守り、次の世代へと引き継いでいかなければならないと思うばかりです。これは私たち建築家の大きな責任です。

　6つの研究課題は、古民家を町づくり、地域おこし、ひいては日本の財産、世界の財産へとつなげていく大きなパワーの根源(こんげん)となると考える私の心の哲学なのです。

building and combined them to create a house.

The seasonal nature of the surrounding area is also an important element of the living environment.

Cherry blossoms are in full bloom in spring, and in summer you can swim in the nearby clear stream for sweetfish fishing and camping. Autumn leaves are hunted, and winter is a romantic snow scene. By taking advantage of the goodness of the mountains and reflecting them in home building, we can see that even the four seasons will become an important element that nurtures human sensibilities and emotions.

On the back of my business card, I wrote "six research assignments" based on these philosophies.

【6 research assignments】

- ● Let's value our town/our village
- ● Let's value old things
- ● Let's make the best of the natural environment
- ● Let's appreciate new things
- ● Let's make use of special skills
- ● Let's take another look at our mind

Isn't it a big loss of Japanese asset that an old folk house where craftsmanship remains is destined to be destroyed and disappear just because it gets old? I just think we must protect these treasures and pass them on to the next generation. This is a big responsibility for us architects.

The six research assignments are the philosophy of my mind, which I think will be the source of great power to build old folk houses into towns, revitalize the area, and eventually contribute them to the assets of Japan and the world.

「古民家ときめき再生」の枠を超えて

Beyond the framework of "Wonder renovation of old folk houses"

◇ 1 　ゆずハウス

　私たちは古民家の枠を越えた地域活動にも力を入れています。ここではそのユニークな取り組みをいくつかご紹介いたします。

　毎年、夏の暑い時期になると、全国のニュースで話題になる渇水（かっすい）問題。
　渇水率の話になると、まるで風物詩（ふうぶっし）のように取り上げられるようになった高知の建造物に早明浦（さめうら）ダムがあります。
　そのダムがある高知県長岡郡本山町（もとやまちょう）に、予約制の貸別荘として私が建てて管理をしている北山山荘（きたやまさんそう）、通称「ゆずハウス」と呼ばれている建物があります。そこに築後 170 年以上たったといわれている茅葺きの庵がありますが、この茅葺きの庵は、私の家づくりの考え方の原点となった建物です。

◇ 1 Yuzu (Lemon) House

We are also focusing on regional activities beyond the scope of old folk houses. Let me introduce some unique activities.

Drought issues are a topic in national news every year during the hot summer season.

When it comes to the drought rate, the Sameura dam is one of the buildings in Kochi that is always mentioned, like a tradition.

In Motoyama-town, Nagaoka-county, Kochi prefecture where the dam is located, there is a building called Kitayama Mountain Lodge known as "Yuzu House", which I built and manage as a reservation-only rental villa. There is a thatched hut that is said to have been built over 170 years ago, and this thatched hut was the starting point of my idea of building a house.

これらの建物の近くに、樹齢100年はあろうかという数本のユズの古木があるので、「ゆずハウス」の名称はそこから名付けました。

　「ゆずハウス」の大きな見どころは、なんと言っても囲炉裏とお風呂です。

　囲炉裏は、茅葺き屋根がある平家建ての建物につくられています。注目してほしいのは梁と柱の部分です。

　百数十年にわたって煙で燻されて、黒光りした梁。これを見ただけでも、この建物の歴史を、ご自身の目で感じ取っていただくことができると思います。

　次に自慢のお風呂をご案内しましょう。

　お風呂はバンガローの1階にあって、太陽熱を利用して灯油を燃料にしている露天風呂です。バンガローそのものも、訪れた人たちに建材の触感の違いを体感してほしくて、2階の床はヒノキの建材に、1階の床はスギの建材にと、あえて材質を変えて使用してあります。

　この下の写真のお風呂は、家を解体した時に不要となった物を野外に据え付けて、屋根を新設しただけの露天風呂？ですが、周囲が緑や岩に囲まれているので爽快感が全く違います。

(4)

　以前に何となく眠りが浅くストレス気味で過度の緊張状態でしたので、この即席の露天風呂に入ったことがありました。

　入浴して3時間足らずで、効果が出てきました。

There are nearly hundred-year-old Japanese Yuzu lemon trees
near these buildings, hence the name "Yuzu House" is derived from
them.

The main attraction of "Yuzu House" is the Irori fireplace and the
bath.

The Irori fireplace is built in a one-story building with a thatched
roof. What I want you to notice is the beams and the columns.

Shiny-black beams have been smoked for over a hundred decades. You can feel the history of this building through your own
eyes just by looking at it.

Next, let me show you my noble bath.

The bath is located on the first floor of the bungalow and is an
open-air bath fueled by kerosene using solar heat. The bungalow
itself has been changed from one material to another, with the second floor being made of Japanese cypress and the first floor being

体の全体がサラサラで、本当にさわやかなリフレッシュ感覚になりました。そして時間の経過とともに、体の芯までたまっていた疲れが、じわじわと融かされていく感じが、いつまでも続いているようでした。

　そんな感覚が夜中まで続き、翌朝は爽快（そうかい）な目覚めができたのです。その感覚を新しいゆずハウスでも味わってもらおうというので作ったのが、前の写真の岩風呂です。（6畳のサンデッキに直接繋がっています）

　この秘密は「自然水」にあります。

「ゆずハウス」の水源は湧（わ）き水ですが特別な成分を含んでいるようで、煮炊（にた）きに使えばご飯や料理が本当においしく、お茶やコーヒー用にしてもおいしく淹（い）れられます。地域に根ざした民家には「地の利」の恵がいっぱいに散らばっているのです。

　まあ、これは個人的な感想になってしまいますが……。

　下の写真はゆずハウスの水源地です。この岩の下の穴の中から水が湧き出ています。命をつなぐ水で、一年中涸（か）れることはありません。

(5)

made of Japanese cedar, in order to make visitors feel the difference in the texture of the building materials.

The bath in the photo (right) is just an open-air bath where a new roof was built and making use of the wasted materials from when the house was demolished. However, it is completely different because it is surrounded by greenery and rocks.

I had a somewhat light sleep, feeling stressed with a high level of tension before, so I had built this open-air bath.

In less than three hours after taking a bath, I felt its effect.

My whole body felt really refreshed. And over time, fatigue that had accumulated in the core of my body seemed to continue to melt gradually.

That feeling lasted through the night, and the next morning I woke up with a refreshed sensation. I wanted to share a taste of that feeling at this new Yuzua House, so I made a rock bath as shown in the previous photo (4). It is directly connected to an 11 square meter size sun deck.

この「自然水」を使っていると、普段は何の気なしに使っている水というものについて、そのありがたさを感じて、大切に使っていかなければならないと改めて思うのです。

　同様に囲炉裏も同じです。主な燃料には薪を使っているのですが、冬に使う薪は、暖かい夏や秋のうちに蓄えておかなければなりません。

　その蓄えている風景や活動も、資源の大切さや、自然の本当の美しさや価値を日常生活の中で自然に学んでいくことができるのです。

　このように、囲炉裏とはまた違った薪ストーブを使うことで、一味違った古民家の雰囲気を演出することができるということもわかっていただけると思います。

The secret lies in the "natural water".

The water vein underneath "Yuzu House" is spring water, but it seems to contain special ingredients. If it is used for cooking, rice and food, which become so delicious, and can be used for making good tea and coffee. The "blessings from the earth" are scattered throughout the private houses rooted in the region.

This is my personal opinion though...

The photo (5) is the water source at Yuzu House. Water is gushing out of the hole under this rock. This life-giving water does not dry out all year round.

When I use this "natural water," I feel the gratitude for water, which I normally use casually, and am reminded that I must use it carefully.

The same applies to the Irori fireplace. The primary fuel is firewood, but the winter firewood must be stored during warm summer and fall.

The landscapes and activities that they store allow us to learn about the importance of resources and the true beauty and value of nature in our daily lives.

In this way, you can also see that by using a firewood stove that is different from the Irori fireplace, you can create different atmospheres in the old folk house.

◆❷◆ **竪穴式住居を作る**

　初心に還る。原点に戻る。そんな意味で、会社の感謝祭のイベントの一環として竪穴式住居を作ったことがありました。

　このような竪穴式住居には、今日の住まいの原点があります。
　共同作業で自分たちのねぐらを作っていく過程で、楽しみながら、何か大切なものを学ぶことができればと思って行いました。
　竪穴式住居は、紀元前2000年前後頃からのもので、現在の農家や民家の住まいの原点にあたるものです。狩猟文化の人類の営みから農耕文化に変わっていく過程で生まれてきたもので、現代の木造住宅の始まりと考えられます。

　私たちはまずは穴を掘り、柱を立て、屋根下地に垂木を組んでいくという順番で作業を進めました。こうした一つ一つの過程の中に、いろんな工夫がなされているのです。
　その竪穴式の住居を、10組の親子と大工さんとで、5回に分けて一緒に作り上げていきました。こうしたかかわりの中で、親子のコミュニケーションはもちろん、住まいの在り方や、自然とのかかわりを学び、自然の素晴らしさや共生、物を大切にする心、そして物を作る喜びを実感していただきたかったのです。

　骨組の上に屋根や壁になる藁を葺いていく作業に取りかかりました。藁は断熱材になり、湿度や煙を住居の隙間から放出しますが、雨風は中に入れないという優れた効果を発揮します。古代の人たちは、こうした竪穴式住居の中で火を囲み、木の実や山菜、肉や魚を焼

◆2◆ Building pit-dwelling house

Remember the spirit that you started with. Return to the origin. In that sense, I once built a pit-house as part of a company's Thanksgiving event.

Such a pit dwelling is the origin of today's housing.

As we worked together to create our own roast, we hoped we could learn something important while enjoying it.

Pit dwellings date back to around 2,000 B.C. and are the origin of today's homes for farmers and private houses. They were born in the process of evolving from a hunting culture to an agricultural culture and are considered to be the beginning of modern wooden houses.

We first dug a hole, erected a pillar, and built a rafter on the roof base. In each of these processes, various ideas were conceived.

Ten pairs of parents and children and a carpenter together built the pit-house dwelling in five sessions. Through these relationships, I wanted them to learn not only about communication between parents and children, but also how to live and how to relate to nature, and to experience the splendor and symbiosis of nature, the spirit of valuing things, and the joy of making things.

いて食事をしていたのです。

　この竪穴式の住居の中に、暖かさが充満しているのを感じられると思います。こうした古代人の生活に思いを馳せるとき、人間として幸せなのは古代なのか現代なのか、果たしてどちらなんだろうと、深く考えさせられます。

　親子が力を合わせる共同作業です。柱を立てると、その柱に梁を掛け、荒縄や木のつるで縛っていきます。

　柱と柱の間に梁を掛け、その梁と柱をしっかりと緊束していきます。この当時から、大工の仕口やホゾ、継ぎ手などが、出来上がってきました。木を仕口で組み合わせた上に、さらに木のつるで固く縛っていくのですから力が必要です。このようにして古代人は、仲間や子どもたちに、行動を通して家の大切さや、命を守ることの重要性

We started thatching the roof and the wall on the frame. Straw provides insulation and releases humidity and smoke through the gaps in the dwelling, but it has the advantage of not allowing rain and wind to penetrate. In ancient times, people surrounded the fire in a pit dwelling and ate their meals by roasting nuts, wild plants, meat and fish.

You can feel the warmth in this pit-house dwelling. When we think about the lives of such ancient people, we are made to think whether we are happy as human beings in ancient times or in modern times.

It's a collaborative effort where parents and children join forces. When you build a pillar, you hang a beam on it and tie it with a rough rope or a vine from a tree.

Hang a beam between the columns and tighten them firmly. From that moment on, a carpenter's wooden joints were developed. It requires strength because the trees are combined at the joint and then tied tightly with the vine of a tree. In this way, the ancient people have shown their friends and children the importance of their home, the importance of saving their lives through

や、人間の本当の幸せが、自分が仲間の役に立ち、喜んでもらうことだと、自然な形で教えてきたのではないでしょうか。

　柱と梁をかけ終わると、次は垂木をかけていきます。足元をしっかりと地面に埋め込み梁と垂木を結わえながら縛っていく作業です。

　その後、土間の中心に穴を掘り、石を並べて囲炉裏を作りました。

　一家がこの囲炉裏を囲んで、食事をしたりコミュニケーションをする大切な場所です。

　不思議なのは、直径 3.3 メートルの小さな住居ですが、出来上がってみるとその空間は、狭くは感じません。いやそれどころか、皆が集まって囲炉裏を囲み団欒をすることで、仲間意識が高まり安心できました。それがどういう訳かわかりませんが、心がホッと癒やされることを知ったのです。

　垂木の根元をしっかりと固めて、雨水が入ってこないように土を盛り、外部への水の流れ道を作ります。こうして自然への対応の仕方を学んでいったのです。

　竪穴式住居の骨組みが完成するとあとは茅を葺くための作業に入りました。

　下地の竹を 40cm ピッチに取り付けて、それにからめて、茅を縄で編んで止めていきます。竪穴式住居では、この茅を大変多く使います。

　先ほども言いましたが、煙や空気は、茅の隙間から抜けていくのに雨水は入ってきません。そして外部の環境は真夏であっても、内部は涼しく冬は暖かいのが本当に不思議です。ここには、素晴らしい先人の知恵が詰め込まれているのです。人間の五感に働きかけて、癒やしと安心感を与えてくれる知恵の宝庫だと言っても過言ではありません。

　このような企画を通して私たちは住まいへの意識、古民家の素晴らしさを学び、広めていく機会をいただいてきたのです。

their actions. Perhaps they have naturally taught that the true happiness of human beings is to help and delight our peers.

Once the pillars and beams are done, the next step is to put up the rafter. It is a work to firmly embed the base in the ground and tie the beams and rafters together.

After that, we dug a hole in the center of the earthen floor, and lined up the stones and made an Irori fireplace.

It is an important place for the family to sit around to eat and communicate.

What's strange is that the small house, 3.3 meters in diameter, doesn't feel small when it is completed. On the contrary, when everyone gathered around the Irori fireplace and had a good time, the sense of fellowship increased. I don't know why, but I knew that my heart would be relieved.

Firmly solidify the roots of the rafters, pour soil to prevent rainwater from entering, and create a water flow path to the outside. We've learned how to cope with nature as such.

After the framework of the pit dwelling was completed, we started to work on thatching.

Attach the backing bamboo in a 40cm pitch and knit straw with a rope to stop it from entangling.

As I said earlier, smoke and air escape through the gaps of straw, but rainwater does not enter. And even in midsummer, it's really strange that the interior is cool and warm in the winter. It's packed with the wisdom from our great ancestors. It is no exaggeration to say that it is a treasure of wisdom that works on the five human senses and gives healing and a sense of security.

Through this project, we have been given the opportunity to learn and spread the sense of housing and excellence of old folk houses.

③ 生輝蔵 いきてるぞう

もう一つ、私が考案したものをご紹介いたします。

木造耐震組み立て式ユニット。その名も「生輝蔵 いきてるぞう」です。

名前は少しふざけているのかもしれませんが、中身は大まじめに作った耐震ユニットです。

これは 2010 年の 7 月に、高知県の経営革新認定企業に 21 日付で認定されました。

室内に置く大きな家具を連想していただけばよいと思います。この蔵は、巨大地震で家が倒壊しても中にいる人間の生命を守ることができるシェルターの機能を果たします。高知県産のスギ・ヒノキをふんだんに使っているため、癒やしの空間として日頃の寝室兼リビング、書斎として機能するように組み上がっています。

もちろん、室外にも設置可能です。3 畳タイプ、4.5 畳タイプ、6 畳タイプと 3 種類ありますので、家の状態に応じて室内外に設置することが可能です。

現在の田舎の耐震性のない古い古民家はほとんど、おじいちゃんおばあちゃんが住んでいます。もちろん、おじいちゃんおばあちゃん

"Ikiteruzo": Alive Shining Warehouse

Let me introduce another building which I designed.

It's an aseismic assembly building named "Ikiteruzo (Alive, Shining, Warehouse)".

The name sounds a bit funny but the content was serious as is a seismic-proof building.

In July 2010, it was certified as a management innovation certified company in Kochi Prefecture dated July 21. I hope you can imagine a big furniture which you put in a room.

This warehouse functions as a shelter that can protect the human lives inside even if the house collapses due to a massive earthquake. Since cedar and Japanese cypress from Kochi Prefecture are used extensively, it is designed to function as a daily bedroom/living room and study, as a healing space.

Of course, it can also be installed outdoors. There are 3 types (3 tatami mats, 4.5 tatami mats, 6 tatami mats) and it can be installed indoor/outdoor according to the conditions of the house.

Most of the old, non-seismic old folk houses in the countryside today are home to grandpas and grandmas. Of course, while grandpas and grandmas are doing well, any house is well managed and maintained.

There are many people who have a strong interest in earthquake reinforcement that protects the house and their own lives. When I talk to such a grandpa and grandma, they always ask me the following.

"When a big earthquake hits, will my house be collapsed and the life will be lost?"

"How much will it cost for the reinforcement?"

高知県経営革新認定企業
高知県指令 22 高商振　第 154 号　（生輝蔵）
Kochi Prefecture Management Innovation Certified
Company　Kochi Prefecture Order 22 No.154 "Ikiteruzo"

の元気な間は家の管理や手入れは細やかに行き届いてしっかりしています。

　その家を守り、合わせて自分の命を守る耐震補強に強い関心を持っている方が大勢います。そんなおじいちゃんおばあちゃんと話をすると、必ずこのようなことが聞かれます。

「このままでは、大きな地震が来た時には、家が崩れて命がなくなってしまう……」

「補強にはどれくらいの金額がかかるの？」

　本当に命を大事にされているのです。ですが、具体的な金額を告げると、悲しそうに……、

「そんなにかかるなら……。なかなかできん……」（そんなに費用が高くなるなら、補強工事はできない……）

　予算を抑え、できるだけ少ない経費で快適な住まいの再生工事をしたいということは、誰もが考えることです。

　おじいちゃんやおばあちゃんの、そうした表情を見るとたまらなくなって、私は何とかならないものかと考え続けました。それが形になったのが「生輝蔵」です。

　催物などの時に見本展示をさせていただいたところ、幸いに非常に好評でした。

They seriously care about their lives. However, when I inform them of the actual cost, they sadly say "If the cost is so high, reinforcement work cannot be done."

Everyone wants to keep their budget down and renovate a comfortable home at the lowest possible cost.

When I saw the grandpa and grandma's facial expressions, I felt very sorry and kept wondering if something could be done. It was "Ikiteruzo" which took shape.

Fortunately, they were very well received when we were given the sample exhibit at an event.

わが町、赤岡

My hometown, Akaoka

風水学的な視点から見ると、高知県は『龍が住み着いて居る場所』といわれているそうです。

龍というのは縁起の良い伝説の架空の生き物ですが、風水学によると龍の気は「波動エネルギー」で、高知県の気候風土がそのエネルギーを持っているそうです。土佐の山並みはくねくねしています。その様は、龍が身をくねらせて喜んでいるように見えますが、これこそ、喜びのエネルギーを表すものだそうです。これは他県にはない高知県の特徴です。

当社の所在地である高知県香南市は、高知龍馬空港から車で東へ約7分の所にあります。夜須町、香我美町、赤岡町、野市町、吉川村の5ヶ町村が合併して、香南市ができたのです。各町村には、それぞれ個性ある山海の珍味や、新鮮な海の幸、山の幸が豊富で、自然の恵みや魅力ある環境に囲まれた豊かな町です。

私の住んでいる赤岡の街筋には今も古い商店の街並みが続いています。ここにはまだまだ味わいのある古きよきものや文化が残っています。

商店主も高齢化して町にはほとんど人通りも少なくなってきてはいますが、そんな今だからこそ、温故知新。人生経験のある生活の知恵を知っている方々が、若い後世の方々に、偉大な文化と生活の智恵と、人とのきずなや優しさを、しっかりと引き継ぎ教えていく転機ではないかと思っているところです。

古民家の雰囲気は本当に魅力的です。一つ一つすべて違った魅力があり個性的です。これは人間と全く同じだと、いつも感心させられるのです。

私の夢は、こうした街並みを生かして、高齢者が生き生きとできる街を温故知新の町を再生していくことです。

古民家を売りの商店にして、店主も高齢者、買い物に来る方々も高

From a feng shui point of view, Kochi Prefecture is said to be the place where dragons live.

The dragon is a legendary fictional creature of a good fortune, but according to the art of feng shui, the dragon's energy is "wave energy," and climate and natural features of Kochi Prefecture has its energy. Mountains of Tosa (Kochi Prefecture) are winding. It looks like the dragon is swaying and happy, but this is what represents the energy of joy. This is a characteristic of Kochi Prefecture that is not found in other prefectures.

Our company is located in Konan-city, Kochi Prefecture, about a 7-minute drive east of the Kochi Ryoma Airport. Yasu-town, Kagami-town, Akaoka-town, Noichi-town, Fukukawa-village merged and became Konan-city. Each town/village has its own unique delicacy and abundant fresh and delicious food from the sea and mountain. It is a rich town surrounded by the blessings of nature and an attractive environment.

The streets of Akaoka, where I live, still have the street of old shops. Good old things and culture still have a good taste here.

Although there are less populated streets due to aging of owners of the shops, I think we're at a turning point that those who have life experiences and a knowhow of living will pass their great culture and life wisdom, human bond and kindness down to younger generations.

The atmosphere of an old folk house is truly attractive. Every house has its own charm and individuality. I'm always impressed that this is exactly like human beings.

My dream is to revitalize a town where elderly people live cheerfully by taking advantage of such town features.

Why not make such an old folk house a shop where the owner is an elderly person and those who come for shopping are also elderly

齢者もしくは、連れ添ってきた若い方々。そこではお互いをいたわり
あう優しさと心遣いがあり、温かいコミュニケーションが生まれます。

　昔にはあって、今はなくなっている大切なものを人生の大先輩から
教えていただく町づくりができるよう。ますます古民家再生に力をい
れていきたいと思うばかりです。

　赤岡には全国的に知られる奇祭「絵金祭り」をはじめ、「どろめ祭
り」近年生まれた「冬の夏祭り」など、昔ながらのさまざまな祭りや
新しいイベントが多くの庶民を交えて行われています。

　全国的に有名な「絵金祭り」は、古くは、香南の商都として栄えた
赤岡の豪商たちが、邪悪を払い、邪悪を寄せ付けないために店の守り
神として、絵金びょうぶ絵（本物）を店先に飾ったのが始まりだった
ようです。

　極彩色で彩られた屏風絵が、商店の軒先に飾られ、夕闇とともにロ
ウソクが灯されると、町は昔懐かしい静かな息吹を取り戻します。全
国から人が集まってくる理由がわかる気がします。

　この絵金祭りの会場となっている赤岡町の商店街の横町に、当社の
リフォーム展示場「えこひ～き」があります。その隣の２階建ての家
が私の自宅です。

　１階部分では、焼きそばや、おでん、ビールなどを、食べていただ
きながら涼しさを味わっていただくために、『四谷怪談』『牡丹灯籠』
という懐かしい怪談の映画を上映したりしています。

　当社のリフォーム展示場、「えこひ～き」は、もと魚屋さんの店舗
を改装して、囲炉裏をつけ加えたものです。古い文化と、古い建物、
その中の古木の多くが、私たちの心に懐かしい郷愁を語りかけてきま
す。

　心を癒やし安心感を与えてくれる伝統の文化には、そんな優しさが
あるんだなと体感していただけることでしょう。

people and accompanied by young people? There is kindness and consideration to caring for each other which creates warm communication.

I just want to put more effort into regenerating old folk houses so that I can create a town where seniors can teach important things that existed in the past and are now gone.

In Akaoka, various traditional festivals such as national-famous strange festival "Ekin Festival" and "Dorome Festival" and the more recently born "Winter Festival" etc. are held with a lot of common people.

It seems that the famous 'Ekin Festival' was started by the wealthy merchants in Akaoka, who had flourished in the commercial capital of Konan in ancient times, who decorated "Ekin-byobu-e, gold folding screen painting" (real) in the entrance of their stores

筆者が描いたものが現在もポスターとして活用いただいています。
The design of the author has been used for the poster until today.

　ここにも県外からの多くの方々が来られます。

　祭りが始まり、夕闇が近づいてくると、だんだん表の人通りが多く
なってきます。そして商店のあちこちで、「これいくら？」「300円で
す」「これください」「はいありがとうございます。お客さんどちらで
すか」「東京からです」「へえ〜東京からですか。よくきてくれまし
た」こうした会話が弾んでいます。日本伝統の文化が育てるコミュニ
ケーションの温かさをつくづくと感じます。

　ところで、この赤岡町の絵金祭りも回を重ねるごとに、いつしか、
貴重な時間が経過してきて、空き店舗が多くなり、古い民家が取り壊

as a guardian deity of the stores in order to rid the evil and keep the evil away.

When the colorful folding screen paintings are displayed on the eaves of the stores and the candles are lit with the dusk, the town regains its nostalgic silent atmosphere. I feel like I can understand why people from all over Japan are coming.

On the first floor, movies of nostalgic ghost stories such as "Yotsuya Kaidan" and "Botan lantern" are screened so that you can enjoy the coolness while eating yakisoba (stir-fried noodles), oden (Japanese food of stewed ingredients), beer, etc.

Our remodeling exhibition hall "Ekohiiki" is a renovated fish store with an Irori fireplace that has been added. Old culture, old building and many of the old wood inside are reminiscent of nostalgia in our hearts.

You will find such kindness in a traditional culture that heal and reassure your heart.

There are guests from outside the prefecture as well.

As the festival begins and the darkness approaches, the streets become more and more crowded. There are conversations here and there at shops "How much is this?" "It's 300 yen." "I'll take this." "Thank you. Where are you from?" "I'm from Tokyo." "Wow, from Tokyo? Welcome!" I feel the warmth of communication nurtured by Japanese traditional culture.

On the other hand, with repetition of Ekin Festival in Akaoka-town, precious time has been passing by and the number of vacant stores has increased, and old private houses have been demolished and becoming vacant lots.

It is truly regrettable that old folk houses, where the skills of these masters remain, are left behind and are destined to disappear just because they are old. It is a huge loss of Japanese assets.

されて空き地となっています。

　こうした匠たちの技が残る古民家が、古くなったという理由だけで取り壊され、消える運命にあるのは本当に残念なことです。日本人の財産の大きな損失です。このすごい宝物を何としても守っていかなければならない。これは私たちの大きな責任でもあると感じています。取り壊される一方で、古民家は俄然(がぜん)注目を浴びています。

　古民家カフェ、古民家ギャラリー、古民家民宿、古民家食堂、古民家酒屋といったように、古民家とインパクトのあるお店や個性ある住まいが融合し、安らぎ、自信と落ち着き、活力と夢が引き出されているのです。

　これらはいずれにしても、今後世界にアピールできる『日本再興(にほんさいこう)』への、大きなキーワードとなっていくのではないでしょうか。古民家に代表される田舎の良さ、都会にはない安らぎ。つまり「田舎力」の真価(しんか)が見直される時期が来るだろうということです。

　時代は日々変化しており、それに伴い価値観にも大きな変化が起きています。

　例えば巨大資本で、金に糸目を付けずに箱物(はこもの)を創る時代は、近い将来に必ず衰退(すいたい)をしていくでしょう。

　私には、情報化社会で便利になり、華やかになっていけばいくほど、人々は精神の安らぎを求めて、精神性のある物、人間の五感に大きな刺激を与えるものに注目が集まり、それらの価値は次第に高まっていく時代を迎えていくように思えてなりません。

　そんな時代に、田舎の果たす役割は今後ますます重要になるでしょう。これからは「田舎カラーこそが、最大の強み」になってくるかもしれません。

　田舎には、まだまだ知られていない未知の価値あるパワーや宝物がたくさん散在(さんざい)しています。精神の慈養(じよう)となる多くの「温故知新」の宝

We must protect great treasures at all costs. I feel it's also our great responsibility.

While being demolished, old folk houses are receiving a lot of attention. Old folk houses are merged with unique shops such as café, gallery, inn, dining, bar, etc., or residences and bring out relaxation, confidence, energy and dreams.

In any case, I think these will become big keywords for "Japan Revitalization" that can appeal to the world in the future. The advantages of the countryside are represented by old folk houses, peace of mind that is not found in the city. It means, there will be a time when real value of the "power of the countryside" will be reassessed.

Times are changing day by day, and along with that, the values are also changing significantly.

For example, an era in which the massive cities create edifices regardless of costs will certainly decline soon.

The more convenient and gorgeous the computerized society would become, the more people would look for peace of mind, and the more spiritual things, and the ones that give a great stimulus to the five human senses would attract attention. It seems that we are entering an era in which such value will gradually increase.

In such an era, the role of the countryside will become more and more important. Rural settings may become the greatest assets in the future.

The countryside is full of unknown and valuable powers and treasures. Many treasures of "discovering new through old wisdom" which nourish our spirit are buried here and there.

I think the time will come when we will polish our old culture, traditions and history untapped in the countryside and make them shine.

物が、あちこちに埋もれているのです。

　田舎に眠る古い文化や伝統や歴史に磨きをかけて、輝かせていく時代が来ると思います。

　古き良き赤岡の町並み。赤岡の商店街の町全体が、古民家が多く、そうした古民家を活用して、独特な雰囲気や空間を創っています。

　「ここに、こんな変わった空間を持った古民家があれば、また一段と町の雰囲気を魅力あるものにすることができる！」そんなことを思うと私はわくわくします。

　地域独特の雰囲気が出て、個性ある町づくりが少ない予算で出来上がることこそ、古民家の最大の特徴です。ぜひ、赤岡に遊びに来てください。そして、古民家の町並みをゆっくりと味わっていただきたいと思います。

Good old Akaoka townscape. The whole shopping district, where many old folk houses exist, has a unique atmosphere and space to be developed.

"If there was an old folk house with such an unusual character here, we could make the atmosphere of our town even more attractive!" I am excited to think about such an idea.

It is the most distinctive feature of the old folk house that it can create a unique atmosphere in an area and a unique town building within a small budget.

Please come and visit Akaoka. I would like you to take time to enjoy the streets of old folk houses.

あとがき

　2013 年 4 月で古民家ときめき再生事業を発足しちょうど 6 年となりました。その間には、県下各地で『古民家ときめき再生事業』のネットワーク設立のための説明会を行って共に再生事業に取り組む参加企業を募りました。こうした事業のネットワーク化が実現すると、古民家や空き家の再生は物件情報から始まり調査の段階から、設計・施工・流通販売・メンテナンス・利用相談・賃貸・管理などなど、トータルなサービスを展開して、お客さまに提供できるようになります。現在、5 社の企業にご参加いただき、古民家ときめき再生事業に取り組み始めたところです。激動の社会を生き延び、新しい流れを作り、かけがえのない文化を育んでいくためには、地元に根づいた土着の大工さんたちと力を合わせていく以外にありません。時代を変える大きな力になりえることを土佐の先人は教えてくれています。今、坂本龍馬の時代を凌ぐ大きな激動の変換点に遭遇している私たちにとっては、新しい発想と理念のもとでの人と人とのネットワークの力を生かす以外に方法はないと思っています。

　前述の『古民家ときめき再生』工事は、生きている資材をできるだけ多く使い、工事を行っていきます。そのために室内の通風や、それぞれの素材の特徴である長所や欠点をよく知ったうえで、適材適所に配置していくことが大事となってきます。

　快適な住まいは、住まう方々との度重なるコミュニケーションから生まれてきます。それは単なる物創りだけでなく、人間の精神性、発展性を見据えたうえで、さらに自然との共生も視野に入れて積み上げていくものです。そのために多くの方々との交流を

Postscript

It's been exactly 6 years since we started the "Wonder Renovation of Old Folk Houses Project" in April 2013. In the meantime, we held briefing sessions for the establishment of a network of "Wonder Renovation of Old Folk Houses Project" in various areas of my prefecture and recruited participating companies to work on the renovation projects together. When such a network of businesses is realized, the renovation of old folk houses and vacant houses starting from the information on the property and the investigation stage, a total service, including design, construction, distribution sales, maintenance, usage consultation, rental, management, etc. can be developed to provide to our customers. Currently, five companies have joined and the project has just started. The only way to survive our turbulent society, always creating new trends, and fostering an irreplaceable culture is to work with indigenous carpenters rooted in the local area. Tosa's predecessors have taught us it can be a great force to change era. As we are now confronted with a great transformation point beyond the time of Ryoma Sakamoto, we believe that there is no other way to do this than to utilize the power of networks of people based on new ideas and principles.

The construction of the herein presented "Wonder Renovation of Old Folk Houses Project" will be carried out using as many living materials as possible. Therefore, it is important to understand the ventilation in the room, the advantages and disadvantages of each material, and then to place the right material in the right place.

A comfortable home is born from repeated communication

一層深め、英知を結集して、わが愛する高知の郷土から、日本の宝物・古民家の力を発信して、温故知新の輪を一層広げていくことを強く願うばかりです。

　家を建てるということは、その家族にとっては一世一代の大事業です。

　子の代や孫の代まで、自分の一族の幸せを考え抜いたうえで家をつくり上げていかなければなりません。それは、夢の実現であり幸せづくりの基本なのです。

　その幸せというものを追求していくと、日々の生活に潤いを取り入れていくことが、非常に大切になってくることに気がつきます。

　ですが、さらにそれを追及するとなると、建物のことだけを考えていては、限界が出てきます。

　そうなると、「衣食住」と言った、いろんな分野にまで考えを広げて、それらに対して、積極的に関わっていく必要性が出てくるのです。

　また、家の中での日常生活において、どれだけ多くの感動を、自分のものにできるかということも課題になってきます。

　それは、自分自らが感動しなければ、相手に伝えることはできません。

　住まいにはいろいろ可能性があり、また、ある程度の遊び心も必要なのです。

　ウキウキワクワクするような空間設計や居場所を、家の内部や外部で考えて見てみると、楽しく個性のある、自分だけのわが家を作り出すことができるかと思います。

　家作りを考えている方や、今住んでいる方も、住まうわが家に

with the people who live in it. It is not just about creating things, but also about looking at human spirituality and development as well as about symbiosis with nature. For that purpose, I strongly hope that we will further deepen exchanges with many people, gather wisdom, transmit the power of Japanese treasures and old folk houses from my beloved hometown of Kochi, and further expand the circle of old and new wisdom.

Building a house is a once-in-a-generation project for any family. You must think about happiness of your family deeply and build a house for your children and grandchildren. It's the realization of dreams and the basis of happiness.

I realize that, as I pursue happiness, it becomes very important to enrich my daily life.

However, when it comes to pursuing it further, there are limits to what you can do if you only think about buildings.

In that case, it will be necessary to expand our thinking to various fields such as "clothing, food and housing" and to be mentally involved in them.

It is also a challenge regarding how much emotion you can bring to your daily life at home.

If you're not moved, you can't convey it to others.

There are various potentials of residences. You need to have a playful mind to some extent.

If you will consider your space design and your living place both inside/outside of your house, I think you can create your own enjoyable unique residence.

Whether you are thinking of building a house or living in a house now, why not try incorporating some new ingenuity and playfulness into your home?

もう一工夫、遊び心というものを取り入れてみてはいかがでしょうか。おそらく、わが家が見違えるほど快適になり、癒やしの居住空間がさらに広がることと思います。そして、それがちょっと無理なようでしたら、せめて、わが家において、自分が一番長い時間いると思われる場所だけでも、快適な空間づくりを目指して実践してみることです。

　これが、家の幸せ度を高めるためには絶対に必要なことだと思います。そして、これらを一つでも作ることができたならば、自分自身はもちろんのこと、家族や来客の方々にも、必ず喜んでいただくことができるようになる。私はそう自負しております。

　私どもの仕事はそのご一家、ご家族の偉大な事業を、一緒になって日々感動し心をときめかせながら手がけさせていただいています。そうした古民家の素晴らしい住まいが一軒でも増えることが願いであります。それ以上の誉れや光栄はありません。

　出版にあたりましては、多くの関係者の方々にご尽力いただきました。特に、古民家の心を十二分に体得されている、エッセイストの渡辺瑠海様には、私のたっての願いで、拙い私の文章に魂を入れていただきました。また、私の建築人生を覚醒させていただいた小原二郎先生ご夫妻には、度重なるご指導をいただきました。ご高齢で療養の身にも関わらず、また、先生ご自身の著作活動を中断をされてまでして、感慨に堪えないご援助をいただき、心遣いやご心配をお掛けして、この本は出来上がりました。ここに心から感謝の意をささげます。

　　2013 年 11 月吉日

　　　　　　　　　　　　　　　　　　片岡　正治

Perhaps it will make your home more comfortable and offer a more relaxing space for living. If it is somewhat impossible, why not try creating a comfortable space at home where you stay for the longest time.

I think it is absolutely necessary to increase the happiness of the house. And if you can even achieve it a little, you will surely be pleased and can make your family and visitors happy. I am sure of it.

Our mission is to work together on the great project of a family while being moved and excited every day. It is my wish that the number of such wonderful old folk houses will increase as much as possible. There is no greater honor for me.

Many people have contributed to this publication. In particular, Ms. Rumi Watanabe, an essayist who has fully mastered the heart of an old folk house, and put her soul into my poor writing at my own request. I also received repeated instructions from Mr. and Mrs. Jiro Ohara, who had awakened my architectural life. I have received impressive support from him while he even suspended his own writing activity in spite of his age and medical treatment. This book was accomplished thanks to his consideration and support. I would like to express my heartfelt gratitude to all.

November 2013

Masaharu Kataoka

プロフィール

片岡　正治　かたおか　まさはる

昭和24年4月　高知県香美郡赤岡町に生まれる。

昭和53年一級建築士資格取得。昭和48年岩城建築設計事務所開設。平成7年MIタウン企画部創設、平成19年「古民家ときめき再生」事業を開始、多くの古民家の再生を手がけ現在に至る。

● 資格取得歴

・一級建築士
・福祉住環境コーディネーター
・ハウジングライフ（住生活）プランナー

H 4. 2.25	財団法人 日本建築防災協会「特殊建築物等調査資格」認定
H19. 8. 1	財団法人 住宅リフォーム・紛争処理支援センター「増改築相談員」
H19.10.24	高知県地球温暖化防止活動推進センター「高知県省エネ住宅アドバイザー」
H21. 4. 1	財団法人 職業技能振興会「古民家鑑定士1級」
H21. 5. 1	一般財団法人 住宅金融普及協会「住宅ローンアドバイザー」
H22. 1.21	社団法人 全国中小建築工事業団体連合会 「住宅瑕疵担保責任保険 ちきゅう住宅検査員」
H22. 6.15	「高知県木造住宅耐震診断士」
H22.10. 1	財団法人 職業技能振興会「伝統資財施工士」
H23. 1.10	一般財団法人 環境マテリアル推進協議会　リフレクティクス仕様工法 「遮熱施工管理士」
H23. 9. 1	「高知県被災建築物 応急危険度判定士」
H23.11.18	財団法人 日本建築防災協会 「震災復旧のための震災建築物被災度区分判定・復旧技術者」
H24.11. 1	公益社団法人 日本木材保存協会「木材劣化診断士」

● 受賞歴

H18. 9.24	高知県木材普及推進協会「第1回もくもくリフォーム王座決定戦」優秀賞
H19	高知県経営革新企業に認定
H20. 2.21	第18回トータルハウジング大賞『リフォーム部門地域最優秀賞』受賞
H21	高知県経営革新支援事業社に決定
H22. 7	第20回トータルハウジング大賞『リフォーム部門地域最優秀賞』受賞
H23. 7. 5	第21回トータルハウジング大賞『リフォーム部門審査員奨励賞』受賞
H24. 7.22	第22回トータルハウジング大賞『リフォーム部門地域最優秀賞』受賞

● ブログ「福運集団の社長奮闘記」

https://blog.goo.ne.jp/mitown_iwaki

翻訳：**佐藤　恵里**（さとう えり）

フレアインターナショナル 代表／全国通訳案内士／ジャパンブランド育成支援事業アドバイザー。1995年に国内外の企業・団体にマーケティング業務を提供するフレアインターナショナルを設立、現在に至る。英語通訳・翻訳をはじめ、日本文化（伝統工芸品／コンテンポラリーアート等）の海外展開支援を続ける。認定NPO法人 Peace Field Japan 副理事長（里山交流団体）

Profile
Masaharu Kataoka

April, 1949   Born in Akaoka-town, Kami-district, Kochi Prefecture.
1973   Established Iwaki Architecture Design Office. 1978   Obtained class-1 architect qualification. 1995   Founded MI Town Planning Department. 2007   Started "Wonder Renovation of Old Folk Houses Project" and has been involved in the renovation of many old folk houses to the present.

● History of Qualification

· Class-1 Architect
· Welfare Environment Coordinator
· Housing Life Planner

Feb. 25, 1992	Japan Building Disaster Prevention Association, "Qualification for investigating special buildings, etc."
Aug. 1, 2007	Center for Housing Renovation and Dispute Settlement Support "Renovation Consultant"
Oct. 24, 2007	Kochi Center for Climate Change Actions "Kochi Prefecture Energy Efficient Housing Advisor"
April. 1, 2009	Vocational Skills Promotion Society "Class-1 Old Folk Houses Appraiser"
May. 1, 2009	General Incorporated Foundation Housing Finance Promotion Association "Housing Loan Advisor"
Jan. 21, 2010	The National Federation of Small and Medium-sized Construction Business Associations, "Housing Defect Liability Insurance, Chikyu (The earth) Housing Inspector"
June. 15,	2010 "Kochi Prefecture Wooden House Seismic Diagnostician"
Oct. 1, 2010	Vocational Skills Promotion Society "Traditional Material Contractor"
Jan. 10, 2011	Environmental Material Innovation Institute, Reflectix specification construction method "Heat Shield Construction Manager"
Sep. 1, 2011	"Kochi-Prefecture Damaged Building Emergency Risk Judge"
Nov. 18, 2011	Japan Building Disaster Prevention Association, "Earthquake disaster building damage classification judgement / recovery engineer for earthquake disaster recovery"

● Award History

Sep. 24, 2006	Kochi Prefecture Wood Promotion Association "The 1st Moku Moku Renovation Championship" Excellence Award
2007	Certified as Kochi-Prefecture Management Innovation Company
Feb. 21, 2008	The 18th Total Housing Grand Prize Awarded "Renovation Division Regional Highest Award"
2009	Determined as Kochi-Prefecture Management Innovation New Support Company
July. 2010	The 20th Total Housing Grand Prize Awarded "Renovation Division Regional Highest Award"
July. 5, 2011	The 21st Total Housing Grand Prize Awarded "Renovation Division Regional Highest Award"
July. 22, 2012	The 22nd Total Housing Grand Prize Awarded "Renovation Division Regional Highest Award"

● Blog "Struggle Diary of the President of Good Fortune Group"

https://blog.goo.ne.jp/mitown_iwaki

Translation : **Eri Sato**

Flair International pounder/National Government Licensed Guide Interpreter/Japan Brand Development Support Project Advisor. Established Flair International in 1995 to provide marketing services to domestic and international companies and organizations, until today, she continues to support the overseas development of Japanese culture (traditional crafts/ contemporary art, etc.) as well as English interpretation and translation.Vice President of Peace Field Japan, a certified NPO (Satoyama exchange organization)

古民家ときめき再生

Wonder Renovation of Traditional Japanese Old Folk House

発行日　2023年12月20日　初版第1刷発行
著　者　片 岡 正 治
翻　訳　佐 藤 恵 里
発行人　坂本圭一朗
発行所　リーブル出版
　　　　〒780-8040　高知市神田2126-1
　　　　TEL 088-837-1250
装　幀　白 石　　遼
印刷所　株式会社リーブル

date of issue : December 20, 2023　first edition

Author : Masaharu Kataoka

Translation : Eri Sato

Publisher : Keiichiro Sakamoto

Publisher : Livre Publishing, 2126-1 Koda, Kochi city, 780-8040
　　　　　　TEL 088-837-1250

Binding : Ryo Shiraishi

Printing : Livre Co., Ltd.